SECOND EDITION

Physical Best Activity Guide

Middle and High School Levels

NATIONAL ASSOCIATION FOR SPORT AND PHYSICAL EDUCATION

HUMAN KINETICS

Library of Congress Cataloging-in-Publication Data

Physical best (Program)
   Physical Best activity guide: middle and high school levels /
National Association for Sport and Physical Education. -- 2nd ed.
      p. cm.
   Includes bibliographical references.
   ISBN 0-7360-4805-7 (soft cover)
   1. Physical education and training--Study and teaching (Secondary) --
United States.   2. Physical education and training--Study and teaching
(Middle school)--United States.   I. National Association for Sport and
Physical Education.   II. Title.
   GV365.P49916   2004
   613.7'071'2--dc22

                                        2004014449

ISBN: 0-7360-4805-7

Acquisitions Editor: Bonnie Pettifor
Developmental Editor: Jennifer Sekosky
Assistant Editor: Ragen E. Sanner
Copyeditor: Christine M. Drews
Proofreader: Kathy Bennett
Permission Manager: Dalene Reeder
Graphic Designer: Robert Reuther
Graphic Artist: Kathleen Boudreau-Fuoss
Photo Manager: Kareema McLendon
Cover Designer: Robert Reuther; **Photographer (cover):** Kelly J. Huff
Photos (interior): Kelly J. Huff, unless otherwise noted
Art Manager: Kelly Hendren
Illustrator (book interior): Accurate Art, Inc.; **Illustrator (CD-ROM):** Keri J. Evans
Printer: United Graphics

Other credits: We would like to thank Stephen Decatur Middle School in Decatur, Illinois, for assistance in providing the location for the photo shoot for this book, and the faculty of Johns Hill Magnet School and Douglas MacArthur High School, both of Decatur, Illinois, for assistance in providing models.

Printed in the United States of America   10 9 8 7 6 5 4 3 2 1

Human Kinetics
Web site: www.HumanKinetics.com

United States: Human Kinetics
P.O. Box 5076, Champaign, IL 61825-5076
800-747-4457
e-mail: humank@hkusa.com

Canada: Human Kinetics
475 Devonshire Road Unit 100
Windsor, ON N8Y 2L5
800-465-7301 (in Canada only)
e-mail: orders@hkcanada.com

Europe: Human Kinetics
107 Bradford Road, Stanningley
Leeds LS28 6AT, United Kingdom
+44 (0) 113 255 5665
e-mail: hk@hkeurope.com

Australia: Human Kinetics
57A Price Avenue, Lower Mitcham
South Australia 5062
08 8277 1555
e-mail: liaw@hkaustralia.com

New Zealand: Human Kinetics
Division of Sports Distributors NZ Ltd.
P.O. Box 300 226 Albany
North Shore City, Auckland
0064 9 448 1207
e-mail: blairc@hknewz.com

CONTENTS

ACTIVITY FINDER

Activity number	Activity title	Activity page	Concept	Middle school	High school	Reproducible (on CD-Rom)
3.1	Aerobic Capture	23	Definition	●		None
3.2	Clean Out Your Arteries	26	Health benefits	●		None
3.3	Aerobic Benefit Hunt	28	Health benefits	●		Aerobic Benefit Cards
						Aerobic Benefit Student Worksheet
3.4	Wanderer	30	Warm-up and cool-down; intensity	●		Heart Rate Record Sheet
3.5	Four-Corner Heart Healthy Warm-Up and Cool-Down	33	Warm-up and cool-down		●	Benefits of Warming Up and Cooling Down Poster
						Four-Corner Heart Healthy Warm-Up and Cool-Down Cards
3.6	Fitting in Fitness	36	Frequency	●		Basketball Handout
						Jogging Handout
						Tennis Handout
						Aerobics Handout
						Football Handout
						Volleyball Handout
						Skating Handout
						Hockey Handout
3.7	Heartbeat Stations	40	Intensity and time	●		Heartbeat Stations Score Sheet
3.8	Cross-Training Trio	42	Time and type	●	●	Aerobic Fitness: Cross-Training Activities Log
						Aerobic Fitness: Cross-Training Benefits and Guidelines
3.9	Target Zone Aerobic Martial Arts	45	Intensity and time		●	Target Zone Aerobic Martial Arts Recording Form
3.10	Continuous Relay	48	Intensity and time		●	Individual Workout Log
4.1	Imposter—Or Not?	56	Definition	●		Imposter—Or Not? Station Task Cards
						Imposter—Or Not? Worksheet
4.2	Go for the Team Gold	59	Health benefits	●		Go for the Team Gold Task Cards
						Go for the Team Gold Handout

(continued)

Activity number	Activity title	Activity page	Concept	Middle school	Hgih school	Reproducible (on CD-ROM)
6.1	Build a Body	107	Definition	•		None
6.2	All Sport Body Comp Quizzo	110	Definition	•	•	Body Composition Quizzo Chart
						Body Composition Quizzo Term Cards
						All Sport Body Comosition Activity List
6.3	Body Comp Survivor	113	Health benefits	•	•	Body Composition Survivor Challenges
						Three Body Composition Puzzles
						Super Survivor Questions
6.4	Frisbee Calorie Blaster	117	Health benefits		•	None
6.5	1,000 Reps	119	Growth and development	•		1,000 Reps and Seconds Chart
						Estimated Energy Expenditure for Common Activities Chart
6.6	Cross-Training Triumph	122	Growth and development		•	Cross-Training Triumph Task Cards
6.7	Health Quest	125	Nutrition	•	•	Checkpoint Signs
						Health Quest Answer Sheets
						Food Guide Pyramid
6.8	Fast Food Frenzy	128	Nutrition	•	•	Fast Food Frenzy Discovery Worksheet
						Calorie Chart
						Instructions for Stations
						Lunch Menu Suggestion Cards
						Health Behavior Contract
6.9	Mass Metabolism	133	Metabolism and nutrition	•		Metabolism Log
7.1	Match the Components	140	Definition	•	•	Health-Related Fitness Activity Cards
7.2	Health-Related, Skill-Related Circuit	142	Definition	•	•	Fitness Components Identification Circuit Instructions
						Fitness Components Identifiction Circuit Worksheet
						Fitness Components Identification Circuit Posters
						Fitness Components Identification Circuit Answer Key

(continued)

Activity number	Activity title	Activity page	Concept	Middle school	High school	Reproducible (on CD-ROM)
10.2	Sticking to a Plan	189	Nonactive versus physically active	●	●	Personal Exercise Word Puzzle
						Fitness Review Crossword Puzzle
						Overcoming Barriers
10.3	Evaluating a Physical Activity Program	192	Evaluation	●	●	Reproducibles for this activity are specific to each Self-Assessment or Activity Idea.
	Self-Assessment Idea: Evaluating Your Physical Activity Program	192	Evaluation	●	●	Evaluating Your Physical Activity Program
	Activity Idea: Perform Your Plan	192	Evaluation and change	●	●	Performing Your Plan
	Activity Idea: Your Exercise Circuit	193	Development	●	●	Your Exercise Circuit
	Activity Idea: Your Health and Fitness Club	194	Evaluation	●	●	Your Health and Fitness Club
	Activity Idea: Heart Rate Target Zones	195	Heart rate and aerobic fitness		●	Aerobic Fitness: How Much Activity Is Enough?
	Activity Idea: Sports Stars	196	Exercise	●	●	Sports Stars Program

PREFACE

Physical Best is a comprehensive health-related fitness education program developed by physical educators for physical educators. Physical Best was designed to educate, challenge, and encourage all young people in the knowledge, skills, and attitudes needed for a healthy and fit life. The goal of the program is to help students move from dependence to independence for their own health and fitness by promoting regular, enjoyable physical activity. The purpose of Physical Best is to educate *all* children, regardless of athletic talent, physical and mental abilities or disabilities. Physical Best implements this goal through quality resources and professional development workshops for physical educators.

Physical Best is a program of the National Association for Sport and Physical Education (NASPE). A nonprofit membership organization of over 18,000 professionals in the sport and physical education fields, NASPE is an association of the American Alliance for Health, Physical Education, Recreation and Dance dedicated to strengthening basic knowledge about healthy lifestyles among professionals and the public. Putting that knowledge into action in schools and communities across the nation is critical to improved academic performance, social reform, and the health of individuals.

Overview of Physical Best Resources

This guide contains the information you need to help 6th- to 12th-grade students gain the knowledge, skills, appreciation, and confidence to lead physically active, healthy lives. The easy-to-use instructional activities have been developed and used successfully by physical educators across the United States. You will find competitive and noncompetitive activities, demanding and less demanding activities, and activities that allow for maximum time on task. Above all, the activities are designed to be educational and fun! Packaged with the book is a CD-ROM containing reproducible charts, posters, and handouts that accompany the activities. New features for the second edition include many new activities in each chapter, the addition of a new chapter, Combined-Component Training, that contains activities incorporating multiple health-related fitness components, and a new section focused on personal health and fitness planning, which introduces students to the skills they'll need to be physically active for life after they graduate from high school.

This book has two companion resources:

■ *Physical Education for Lifelong Fitness: The Physical Best Teacher's Guide, Second Edition* is a comprehensive guide to successfully incorporating health-related fitness and lifetime physical activity into physical education programs. The guide provides a conceptual framework based on recent research, covering topics such as behavior, motivation and goal setting, health-related fitness curriculum development and teaching methods, components and principles of fitness, and inclusion in health-related fitness, and health-related fitness assessment. The guide also contains a wealth of practical information and examples from experienced physical educators. The second edition has streamlined and reorganized many of the chapters, added a glossary and more practical information and resources for physical educators, and updated information and references throughout the text.

■ *Physical Best Activity Guide: Elementary Level, Second Edition* contains the information needed to help K-5 students gain the knowledge, skills, appreciation, and confidence to lead physically active, healthy lives. The easy-to-use instructional activities have been developed and used successfully by physical educators across the United States. You will find competitive and noncompetitive activities, demanding and less demanding activities, and activities that allow for maximum time on task. Above all, the activities are designed to be educational and fun! Packaged with the book is a CD-ROM of reproducible charts, posters, and handouts that accompany the activities, many new activities in each chapter, a sample newsletter for each component of fitness, and a new chapter titled Special Events, which contains activities that coincide with national holidays and health observances throughout the school year.

Related Resources

During a typical school year, many educators will use more than one program and a variety of teaching resources, overlapping different approaches on a day-to-day basis. With this in mind, it may be reassuring to know that although Physical Best is designed to be used independently for teaching health-related fitness, the following resources can also be used in conjunction with the Physical Best program. *FITNESSGRAM/ACTIVITYGRAM*, *Fitness for Life* and the NASPE products listed in the next section are suggested resources to complement Physical Best.

FITNESSGRAM/ACTIVITYGRAM

FITNESSGRAM/ACTIVITYGRAM is a comprehensive health-related fitness and activity assessment and computerized reporting system. All elements within *FITNESSGRAM/ ACTIVITYGRAM* are designed to assist teachers in accomplishing the primary objective of youth fitness programs, which is to help students establish physical activity as a part of their daily lives.

FITNESSGRAM/ACTIVITYGRAM promotes the belief that regular physical activity contributes to good health, improved function, and overall well-being and that it is important throughout a person's lifetime. This assessment encourages school programs to have the long-term view of promoting appropriate physical activity rather than focusing only on testing and performance aspects of physical fitness in children and youth. Physical activity should be fun and enjoyable.

FITNESSGRAM/ACTIVITYGRAM resources are published and available through Human Kinetics, as are the Brockport Physical Fitness Test, which is a health-related fitness assessment for students with disabilities.

Fitness for Life

Fitness for Life is a complete set of resources for teaching a lifetime fitness and wellness course at the secondary level. It is compatible with the Physical Best program in philosophy, with the goal of lifelong physical activity habits, and *Fitness for Life* is a program that has been shown by research to be effective in promoting physically active behavior after students finish school.

Fitness for Life and Physical Best complement one another effectively, because the *Physical Best Activity Guide: Middle and High School Levels, Second Edition* can be used both before and after a *Fitness for Life* course, as well as during the course to provide supplemental activities. Both programs are based on the HELP philosophy, which promotes health for everyone with a focus on lifetime activity of a personal nature. In fact, the two programs are so compatible that the Physical Best program offers teacher training for *Fitness for Life* course instructors.

NASPE Resources

NASPE publishes many additional useful and related resources that are available by calling 800-321-0789 or online through the AAHPERD store at www.aahperd.org.

- *Moving Into the Future: National Standards for Physical Education, Second Edition.*
- *Beyond Activities: Learning Experiences to Support the National Physical Education Standards*
- *Appropriate Practices Documents (Elementary, Middle School, and High School)*
- Assessment Series—titles relating to fitness and heart rate
- *Physical Activity for Children: A Statement of Guidelines for Children Ages 5-12.*

Physical Best Certification

Physical Best provides accurate, up-to-date information and training to help today's physical educators create a conceptual and integrated format for health-related fitness education within their programs. NASPE/AAHPERD offers a certification program that allows physical education teachers to become Physical Best Health-Fitness Specialists. The Physical Best certification has been created specifically for the purpose of updating physical educators on the most effective strategies for helping their students gain the knowledge, skills, appreciation, and confidence needed to lead physically active, healthy lives. The program focuses on application—how to teach fitness concepts through developmentally and age-appropriate activities.

To earn certification through NASPE/AAHPERD as a Physical Best Health-Fitness Specialist, you will need to do the following:

- Attend the one-day Physical Best Health-Fitness Specialist Workshop.
- Read this book, *Physical Education for Lifelong Fitness: The Physical Best Teacher's Guide, Second Edition*, and the *FITNESSGRAM/ACTIVITYGRAM Test Administration Manual, Third Edition.*
- Using the required resources mentioned above, complete a take-home examination and submit it to NASPE/AAHPERD. Successful and timely completion and submission to NASPE/AAHPERD will result in certification.

For more information or to learn about becoming a Physical Best Health-Fitness Specialist or Instructor (to train other teachers), call Physical Best at 800-213-7193.

ACKNOWLEDGMENTS

Many educators contributed their time and expertise to this project, beginning with reviews of the first edition by many of the Physical Best Steering Committee members and Physical Best Instructors from around the country. We would like to thank Marian Franck (Maryland), who wrote the report for this book, synthesizing feedback from multiple sources and detailing a comprehensive list of recommendations for the second edition.

In addition to the overall guidance of the Physical Best Steering Committee, the following individuals contributed new activities or significant editorial input for this edition:

Melissa Black
Ohio

Jeff Carpenter
Washington

Charles Corbin
Arizona

Darren Dale
Connecticut

Paul Darst
Arizona

Gary Feltman
Illinois

Jennie Gilbert
Illinois

Linda Hilgenbrinck
Illinois

Jill Humann
New Jersey

John Kading
Wisconsin

Margaret Kading
Wisconsin

Melody Kyzer
North Carolina

Judy Jagger-Mescher
Ohio

Nila Ledford
Maryland

Guy LeMasurier
Pennsylvania

Ray Martinez
Wisconsin

Carolyn Masterson
New Jersey

Karen McConnell
Washington

Jennifer Melnick
Maryland

Margie Miller
Missouri

Cindy Mitchell
Washington

Cynthia Naylor
Maryland

Kevin O'Brien
Ohio

Sarajane Quinn
Maryland

Mary Jo Sariscsany
California

Hosung So
California

Belinda Stillwell
California

Kathleen Thornton
Maryland

Linda Webbert
Maryland

Christopher Wunder
Maryland

Elizabeth Zinkand
Maryland

An extra note of thanks goes to Charles Corbin, Darren Dale, Guy LeMasurier, and Karen McConnell, for their work on the new section "Personal Fitness Connections"; to Jeff Carpenter, Jennie Gilbert, John Kading, Margaret Kading, Judy Jagger-Mescher, Ray Martinez, and Kevin O'Brien who greatly assisted in the review and editing stage; and to Linda Hilgenbrinck and Gary Feltman for editing and contributing to the new "Inclusion

Tips" portion of each activity. Thanks also to Gayle Claman, professional services manager for Physical Best, who played a significant role in coordinating the revision.

Sponsorship

NASPE would like to thank Mars, Inc., and FlagHouse/Cateye Fitness (official equipment sponsor) for their financial and developmental support of the Physical Best program.

The Physical Best program has been reviewed by the American Heart Association and is consistent with their science and recommendations for physical activity.

© 2004 American Heart Association, Inc.

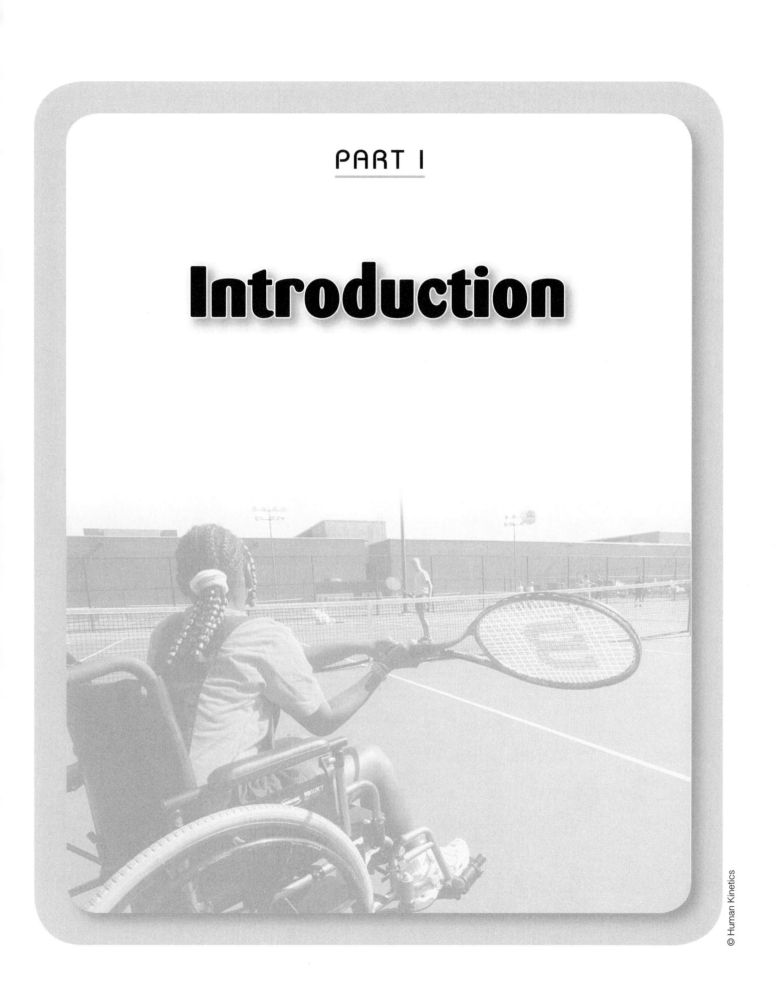

PART I

Introduction

Teaching Middle and High School Level Health-Related Fitness

Chapter Contents

© Human Kinetics

For foundation in teaching health-related fitness activities, we look first to national standards. Many of the national standards that have been developed for physical education, health, and dance can be applied to teaching health-related fitness activities. In the first part of this chapter, we list the national standards from these areas and emphasize the standards that are addressed most often when teaching health-related fitness.

The chapter ends with a brief summary of how Physical Best can be incorporated in a physical education curriculum at the middle and high school levels and a detailed look at the Physical Best activity template. All of the activities in this book follow this template, and the explanations provided in this chapter will help you choose the right activity for the right group of students. You can also use this template as a guide for developing your own activities.

National Standards for Physical Education

The national standards for physical education are based on the definition of the physically educated person as defined in *Outcomes of Quality Physical Education Programs* (NASPE 1992). According to this document, a physically educated person

- has learned skills necessary to perform a variety of physical activities;
- is physically fit;
- participates regularly in physical activity;

National Standards for Physical Education

Physical activity is critical to the development and maintenance of good health. The goal of physical education is to develop physically educated individuals who have the knowledge, skills, and confidence to enjoy a lifetime of healthful physical activity. A physically educated person:

Standard 1
Demonstrates competency in motor skills and movement patterns needed to perform a variety of physical activities.

Standard 2
Demonstrates understanding of movement concepts, principles, strategies, and tactics as they apply to the learning and performance of physical activities.

Standard 3
Participates regularly in physical activity.

Standard 4
Achieves and maintains a health-enhancing level of physical fitness.

Standard 5
Exhibits responsible personal and social behavior that respects self and others in physical activity settings.

Standard 6
Values physical activity for health, enjoyment, challenge, self-expression and/or social interaction.

■ knows the implications of and the benefits from involvement in physical activities; and

■ values physical activity and its contributions to a healthful lifestyle.

NASPE intended for all five parts of the definition "not be separated from each other" (NASPE 1992, p. 6). The definition was further delineated into 20 outcome statements. The definition and outcome statements were used as the basis for the development of the National Standards for Physical Education, originally published by NASPE in 1995 and revised in 2004. The standards define what a student should know and be able to do as a result of a quality physical education program.

So, although all physical education standards are taught to some extent through and during health-related fitness education, two standards are most emphasized:

Standard 3: Participates regularly in physical activity

Standard 4: Achieves and maintains a health-enhancing level of physical fitness

National Health Education Standards

The National Health Education Standards (Joint Committee on National Health Education Standards 1995) are linked to the physical education standards. Health education affords unique knowledge about health, preventing disease, and reducing risk factors in all situations and settings—and it helps to influence behaviors that promote these aims.

National Health Education Standards

Standard 1
Students will comprehend concepts related to health promotion and disease prevention.

Standard 2
Students will demonstrate the ability to access valid health information and health-promoting products and services.

Standard 3
Students will demonstrate the ability to practice health-enhancing behaviors and reduce health risks.

Standard 4
Students will analyze the influence of culture, media, technology, and other factors on health.

Standard 5
Students will demonstrate the ability to use interpersonal communication skills to enhance health.

Standard 6
Students will demonstrate the ability to use goal-setting and decision-making skills to enhance health.

Standard 7
Students will demonstrate the ability to advocate for personal, family, and community health.

Reprinted from *Achieving health literacy: National health education standards* (1995) with permission from the American Alliance for Health, Physical Education, Recreation, and Dance (AAHPERD), 1900 Association Drive, Reston, VA 20191-1599.

Such behaviors include not only physical activity but also other areas of personal, family, and community life.

Health standards 1, 3, and 6 are most closely related to fitness education.

Standard 1: Students will comprehend concepts related to health promotion and disease prevention.

Standard 3: Students will demonstrate the ability to practice health-enhancing behaviors and reduce health risks.

Standard 6: Students will demonstrate the ability to use goal-setting and decision-making skills to enhance health.

National Standards for Dance Education

The National Standards for Dance Education (NDA 1996) are also linked to physical education. Dance is both a movement form (as are sports, aquatics, fitness activities, and outdoor recreational activities) and a form of physical activity that provides health and fitness benefits. Its uniqueness as a physical activity, however, is that it is also an art form, affording opportunities to create, communicate meaning, and interpret cultural issues and historical periods.

For the purpose of these materials, standard 6 is of primary importance in health-related fitness education.

Standard 6: Making connections between dance and healthful living

National Standards for Dance Education

What every young American should know and be able to do in dance:

Standard 1
Identifying and demonstrating movement elements and skills in performing dance

Standard 2
Understanding choreographic principles, processes, and structures

Standard 3
Understanding dance as a way to create and communicate meaning

Standard 4
Applying and demonstrating critical and creative thinking skills in dance

Standard 5
Demonstrating and understanding dance in various cultures and historical periods

Standard 6
Making connections between dance and healthful living

Standard 7
Making connections between dance and other disciplines

National Dance Standards 1-7 (pp. 6-9) – These quotes are reprinted from the *National Standards for Arts Education* with permission of the National Dance Association (NDA) an association of the American Alliance for Health, Physical Education, Recreation and Dance. The source of the National Dance Standards (*National Standards for Dance Education: What Every Young American Should Know and Be Able to Do in Dance*) may be purchased from: National Dance Association, 1900 Association Drive, Reston, VA 20191-1599; or telephone (703) 476-3421.

Integrating the national standards in physical education, health, and dance provides an important way to promote the effects of physical activity on health and one's personal choice to be physically active. None of these disciplines stands alone. Few student groups are solely focused on just one purpose, whether in health, competition, or aesthetics. Although some students have greater interest or aptitude in one of these areas, all youngsters benefit from learning and applying all of these standards. Recognizing these interdisciplinary links helps us maximize our energies for teaching and learning the essential content of three disciplines.

Integrating Physical Best Into the Middle and High School Physical Education Curriculum

The *Physical Best Activity Guide: Middle and High School Levels, Second Edition* is more than a compilation of activities to use with students during their physical education classes. It is designed to help physical education teachers better instruct students, throughout the grade 6–12 physical education curriculum, about being physically fit and physically active for a lifetime. The activities build upon the elementary level book by reinforcing health-related fitness behaviors and concepts. Middle and high school students also learn skills, strategies, and behaviors to assume responsibility for their own physical fitness levels and to attain lifetime fitness.

Physical Best activities vary in length of time to complete and can further vary depending on such aspects as class size and modifications that may be needed according to classroom environment. Because the activities vary in length, you can combine several activities to create one lesson, or you can incorporate individual activities into other lesson plans and units. Students participate in activities that are fun, engaging, and purposeful and at the same time learn about the principles of training, the components of health-related fitness, and the importance of being physically active. Reproducibles on the CD-ROM provide visual aids and extensions of the activities to help students better understand the concepts taught. Finally, students begin to develop strategies and design activities that make them healthier and yet correspond to their particular needs and interests.

Practicing the *FITNESSGRAM* assessments and the Physical Best activities throughout the year helps students learn about their physical fitness levels and what it takes to become healthier. Moreover, the Physical Best program instructs teachers to involve students in physical activity outside of school. The Presidential Active Lifestyle Award (PALA) is endorsed by Physical Best and given by the President's Council on Physical Fitness and Sports to recognize the importance of performing fun fitness activities in and outside of school. Students record how much physical activity they perform on their own or with their friends, family members, and others in the local community. More information on teaching strategies for health-related fitness can be found in *Physical Education for Lifelong Fitness: The Physical Best Teacher's Guide, Second Edition*. Information on the PALA can be found at: www.presidentschallenge.org.

Physical Best Activity Template

Activities that help students learn while doing are the most successful for teaching lifelong fitness. The *Physical Best Activity Guides* provide a wealth of activities designed specifically to help students learn through doing. These activities provide a great start to developing an excellent program, but you'll want to add more activities especially suited for your students.

Following is a step-by-step explanation of the Physical Best activity template, which can also serve as a guide for developing your own activities.

LEVEL

Carefully consider the level of the students for whom you are developing the activity. You can easily modify many activities up or down for students of varying ages and abilities.

CONCEPT

The activity teaches one or more concepts, written in language appropriate to the level of the students. Physical Best includes activities for defining the component of fitness and teaching the health benefits for that component, for warm-up and cool-downs, the FITT Guidelines, and progression and overload. (Chapters 8-10 follow a slightly different format but still list the concept or concepts taught.)

PURPOSE

This component of the template states the student-centered objectives, describing what you want the students to learn.

RELATIONSHIP TO NATIONAL STANDARDS

This component explains which of the national standards in physical education, health education, and dance education the activity addresses.

EQUIPMENT

This component lists everything needed to conduct the activity.

REPRODUCIBLE

This section lists what can be found on the accompanying CD-ROM to support the activity. These are usually charts, signs, task cards, student worksheets, and so forth. You are encouraged to print out the reproducibles that appear on the CD-ROM. They are created for letter-sized paper, but can be enlarged according to your needs. Each is labeled by activity number and reproducible title to help you keep them organized.

PROCEDURE

This component lists steps to conduct the activity, including an introduction (called set-induction in the first edition), activity steps and directions, and closure.

TEACHING HINTS

This component of the template offers ideas for variations, extensions, and increases or decreases in level (for example, notes about intensity, ability groupings, and challenges), as well as safety tips and other ideas for effectively teaching the activity.

SAMPLE INCLUSION TIPS

This component offers one or more tips for adapting the activity to meet the needs of students with varying abilities and health concerns. Note that a tip for one activity may very well be useful for other activities.

ASSESSMENT

This component explains how you or the students will know that they have learned the information stated in the purpose. Assessment may include teacher discussion, student feedback and review, homework assignments, and so on.

Summary

When you use Physical Best, you are teaching the applicable standards through activity in an age-appropriate and sequential manner. Fully utilizing the activity template will ensure that your activities are educational and easy to administer. Choose activities that fit into your lesson plans, and you will teach and reinforce important fitness concepts throughout the year. Most importantly, these activities have been developed by physical educators for physical educators, and so they have been "real world tested" to ensure that they not only teach the concepts, but also allow your students to have fun while performing physical activity.

CHAPTER

2

Introduction to Health-Related Fitness Concepts

Chapter Contents

- Health-Related Fitness

  Principles of Training
  FITT Guidelines
  The Activity Session

- Summary

© Human Kinetics

This chapter introduces the principles of health-related fitness education. An introduction to the components of health-related fitness found at the beginning of each chapter in part II serves as a quick reference when teaching the activities in that chapter. For in-depth study and explanation of these concepts, refer to *Physical Education for Lifelong Fitness: The Physical Best Teacher's Guide, Second Edition*. The new edition includes several new concepts that differ from those in the previous edition, especially in the chapter on aerobic fitness.

Health-Related Fitness

In teaching health-related fitness, we should not lose sight of the importance of physical activity and the development of fun activities that encourage children to be active. Physical Best has consistently emphasized the development of physical fitness as a lifelong process of having an active lifestyle rather than actually being physically fit or attaining a particular performance outcome. The focus of our lessons should be on reinforcing basic concepts and skills ideally taught at the elementary level, and emphasizing the value of physical activity so that students will be competent to participate in activities now and in the future.

Research points to three main reasons children participate in leisure-time activity and sports (Weiss 2000):

■ The development and demonstration of physical competence (athletic skills, fitness, physical appearance)

■ Social acceptance and support from friends, peers, and significant adults

■ Participation in fun activities promoting positive experiences

As you use the Physical Best materials, keep the following definitions in mind to assist you in motivating your students to become physically active, thereby initiating the long path to lifetime fitness and associated health benefits. *Physical fitness* is defined as a set of attributes that people have or achieve relating to their ability to perform physical activity, whereas *physical activity* is defined as any bodily movement produced by muscle contraction that increases energy expenditure (USDHHS 1996; NASPE 2004b). Because motivation for adolescents to be physically active does not come from knowing and appreciating the health benefits of increased activity, you should impress on students that being physically active enables them to have more energy for leisure activities.

Principles of Training

The *overload principle* states that a body system must perform at a level beyond normal to adapt and improve physiological function and fitness. You can increase the overload by manipulating the frequency, intensity, or duration (time) of an activity. To explain overload to adolescents, let them experience it firsthand—keep track of the number of minutes they can sustain an activity or how many repetitions they can perform. You may use a backpack with books or weights and monitor heart rate without the backpack and then with the backpack, explaining how the body will adapt to the heavy load and later be able to do the same load with less effort.

Progression refers to *how* a person should increase the overload. The person should gradually increase the level of exercise by manipulating the frequency, intensity, time, or a combination of all three exercise components. Students should understand that improving their level of fitness is an ongoing process.

Emphasize that all progression must be gradual to be safe. If the overload is applied too soon, the body does not have time to adapt and the benefits may be delayed or an injury may occur. Either result can discourage or prevent a child from participating. For example, a student may progress from performing a reverse curl-up, in which he or she focuses on lowering the body, and work toward performing a regular curl-up. The same strategy works well with push-ups. The student first focuses on the lowering phase. As he progresses he will gain strength to perform the complete push-up. The objective is to challenge students but also create opportunity for success.

To help them understand progression and see that they are improving, give adolescents opportunities to track their progress by keeping a journal. You can also help them understand progression through the use of pretests and posttests.

Specificity states that explicit activities targeting a particular body system must be performed to bring about fitness changes in that area. For example, you must perform aerobic activities that stress the cardiorespiratory system if you want to improve aerobic fitness. This principle applies to all areas of health-related and skill-related fitness, and it applies within a single area of fitness. For example, performing a biceps curl will increase the strength of the biceps muscle but will have no effect on the leg muscles.

The premise behind the *regularity principle* is based on the old adage "use it, or lose it." We lose any fitness gains attained through physical activity if we do not continue to be active. Recognize that the body needs limited recovery time between bouts of exercise. Too little recovery time may lead to injury or overtraining, and too much time between activity sessions can lead to detraining, or loss of the acquired benefits of physical activity and fitness. The recommended time of recovery also varies by area of health-related fitness. For example, the American College of Sports of Sports Medicine (ACSM) recommends three alternate days per week for strength and endurance activities, whereas daily activity is best for improving flexibility. Likewise, the minimum frequency for aerobic improvement is three days per week, and aerobic activity five to seven days per week is optimal. Try to emphasize consistency in activity. Unless you are coaching athletes, do not stress training and conditioning. Remember that recommendations for children's physical activity include daily activity, a recommendation different from that of the traditional ACSM adult model.

The *individuality principle* takes into account that each person begins at a different level of fitness, has personal goals and objectives for physical activity and fitness, and has different genetic potential for change. Although changes in children's physiological responses to training and conditioning are often difficult to measure because of confounding changes associated with normal growth and maturation, recognize that students in your classes will respond differently to the activities you prepare for class. Some will improve, some will not. Some will enjoy the activities, others will not. Your job is to provide plenty of choice in your classroom, taking into account each student's initial fitness level and personal goals.

FITT Guidelines

Physical Best activities apply the FITT Guidelines to improve health and fitness. The acronym FITT describes the frequency (how often), the intensity (how hard), the time (how long), and the type (what kind) of activity necessary for improving and maintaining fitness. The FITT Guidelines also provide the recipe for safely applying the previously described principles of training. Refer to the *Physical Education for Lifelong Fitness: The Physical Best Teacher's Guide, Second Edition* for detailed explanations of the FITT Guidelines and new recommendations concerning their use with students.

The Activity Session

Whether you are teaching kindergarteners or high school seniors, share the purpose of the lesson and how the day's activity will help them reach class goals or personalized goals. Every activity should incorporate a systematic approach to ensure safety and prepare the body for the rigors of the workout. The main physical activity must also be developmentally appropriate for students to feel and understand, through participation, the importance of being physically active. Incorporate cool-down time and use it to review and assess learning.

Summary

Give middle and high school students a variety of activities to choose from, and allow them the opportunity to engage in and appreciate the value of physical activity both now and in the future. Keep in mind that fitness is a journey, not a destination, and that the goal is to progress toward self-assessment and self-delivery of health-related fitness activities. Are you and your students ready for the fun of leading a physically active life? If so, progress to the activities that follow.

PART II

Activities

CHAPTER

3

Aerobic Fitness

Chapter Contents

- Defining Aerobic Fitness
- Teaching Guidelines for Aerobic Fitness
- Training Methods for Aerobic Fitness
- Motor Skill Development Through Aerobic Fitness
- Activities

© Human Kinetics

At the middle and high school levels, we begin to teach and incorporate the adult exercise prescription model in our lessons. However, do not lose sight of implementing fun activities to enhance the quality and productivity of every student's life through physical education. Your goal is to present information that leads to the development of lifelong learners who appreciate and participate in physical activity, both now and in the future. If students understand why these activities are important and how they will benefit from physical activity, they are more likely to take responsibility for becoming physically educated people.

Defining Aerobic Fitness

Aerobic fitness is the "ability to perform large muscle, dynamic, moderate to high intensity exercise for prolonged periods" (ACSM 2000, p. 68). Many field tests are available to assess aerobic fitness. Physical Best endorses *FITNESSGRAM/ACTIVITYGRAM* (The Cooper Institute 2004). The Brockport Test (Winnick and Short 1999) may be used with students with disabilities.

Many health benefits are associated with physical activity (USDHHS 1996; Blair et al. 1995; Boreham et al. 1997; and Boreham et al. 2001). A recent report by the California Department of Education (2002) indicated that higher levels of fitness in children were associated with higher levels of academic performance on standardized testing, supporting the concept that increased physical activity may help to increase a student's capacity for learning (USDHHS 1996). To enhance understanding, you must connect the benefits to something that students can relate to and experience personally and immediately (such as having more energy). The following are potential health benefits of physical activity:

- Strengthens the heart (lower resting and working heart rate, faster recovery)
- Decreases blood pressure
- Strengthens muscles and bones
- Increases energy (for work or leisure activity)
- Allows performance of more work with less effort (get through the day without becoming tired)
- Reduces stress and tension (get along better with others)
- Enhances appearance and feeling of well-being; improves quality of life
- Improves ability to learn (get homework done faster)
- Promotes healthy body composition
- Increases self-confidence and self-esteem (greater social opportunities)
- Enhances sleep
- Improves lipid profile (increases HDL [good cholesterol], decreases triglycerides)
- Helps weight control

Teaching Guidelines for Aerobic Fitness

Teach fitness concepts through physical activity, minimizing classroom lessons where students are inactive. Encourage students to synthesize material presented in class and from outside readings and to make practical applications of the concepts to their personal lives. Circuits or station activities provide excellent opportunity to challenge students independently, refine motor skills, and develop health-related fitness. Keep your groups small and no larger than five at a station. Activities for middle and high school students should include challenges, decision-making skills, and team-building skills. Students at this level should begin to develop and personalize their own fitness programs, recognizing the effect that physical activity has across the lifespan. In selecting and performing activities, follow the training principles outlined in chapter 5 of *Physical Education for Lifelong Fitness: Physical Best Teacher's Guide, Second Edition* to develop aerobic fitness.

Unlike students at the elementary level, where the use of target heart rates is inappropriate, students at the middle and high school level should develop the skills to calculate target heart zones and incorporate them into a personalized fitness program. Expect most students in seventh grade and up to calculate target heart rate values, but avoid the use of target heart rate zones as requirements for participation in physical activity in middle school or junior high. A detailed explanation of the use of target heart rate zones in children appears in chapter 5, "Aerobic Fitness," in the *Physical Education for Lifelong Fitness: Physical Best Teacher's Guide, Second Edition*. The explanation focuses on the fact that adolescents' maximal heart rates are age independent (Rowland 1996), and the traditional target heart rate calculation will not yield the appropriate heart rate required for training and conditioning to gain aerobic fitness.

Remember, we should not be training and conditioning our students, but instilling the importance of physical activity across the lifespan. Ultimately, if adolescents increase physical activity patterns (the process), then fitness (the product) will follow. Young people lose interest in activity if it is not fun. Xiang, McBride, Guan, and Solomon (2003) suggested "when learning tasks are perceived as interesting, relevant, and meaningful, providing opportunities for success, and enhancing ability, students will be motivated to engage in them."

Also note that the formula for calculating maximal heart rate has changed. Although the old formula was simpler to use, it generally overpredicted maximal heart rate (MHR) in those 20 to 40 years of age and underpredicted MHR in those over 40 years of age (Tanaka, Monahan, and Seals 2001). Although students fall outside the ranges of overprediction and underpreduction of MHR using the old formula, the new formula is recommended, and is $MHR = 208 - (.7 \times age)$. Table 3.1 provides information on applying the FITT Guidelines for adolescents (11 years and older) and older youth participating in athletics.

Training Methods for Aerobic Fitness

The three main training methods for developing and maintaining aerobic fitness are continuous training, interval training, and circuit training.

- *Continuous training* is the same activity performed over an extended period. Use caution with this type of activity, because it can become boring and deter students from physical activity rather than promote physical activity. *Fartlek*, a modification of continuous training, intersperses periods of increased intensity with continuous activity over varying natural terrain. This type of activity can be modified and used at all grade levels, but to avoid the "training" aspect as in coaching cross country, allow the students to vary the intensity of some segments.

- *Interval training* involves alternating short bursts of activity with rest periods. Use caution and build variety and skill into the intervals you develop. Do not treat this activity as a practice session for track and field.

- *Circuit training* involves several different activities, allowing you to vary the intensity or type of activity as students move from station to station. It is an excellent method for creating variety and stimulating student motivation. Students at the middle and high school level may enjoy developing stations and circuit-training activities.

TABLE 3.1   FITT Guidelines Applied to Aerobic Fitness

	Adolescents (11+ years)[a]	Middle and high school youth who participate in athletics[b]
Frequency	• Daily or nearly every day • Three or more sessions per week	5 or 6 days per week
Intensity	• Moderate to vigorous activity. Maintaining a target heart rate is not expected at this level. • 12-16 rating of perceived exertion (RPE)[c]	• 60-90% heart rate max (HR max) or 50-85% heart rate reserve (HRR) • 12-16 rating of perceived exertion (RPE)[c]
Time	• 30-60 min daily activity • 20 min or more in a single session	20-60 min
Type	• Play, games, sports, work, transportation, recreation, physical education, or planned exercise in the context of family, school, and community activities • Brisk walking, jogging, stair climbing, basketball, racket sports, soccer, dance, lap swimming, skating, lawn mowing, and cycling	Activities that use large muscles and are used in a rhythmical fashion (e.g., brisk walking, jogging, stair climbing, basketball, racket sports, soccer, dance, lap swimming, skating, and cycling)

[a]Corbin, C .B., and Pangrazi, R. P. (2002). *Physical actvity for children: How much is enough?* In G.J. Welk, R.J. Morrow, and H.B. Falls (Eds), *FITNESS-GRAM reference guide* (p. 7 Internet Resource). Dallas, TX: The Cooper Institute.

[b]American College of Sports Medicine. (2000). *ACSM's guidelines for exercise testing and prescription. 6th ed.,* (Philadelphia: Lippincott, Williams, and Wilkins).

[c]Borg, G. (1998). *Borg's perceived exertion and pain scales* (Champaign, IL: Human Kinetics), 47.

Motor Skill Development Through Aerobic Fitness

Do not underestimate the importance of skill development. Incorporate outdoor skills, team sports, and individualized fitness activities into the lessons. Physical Best activities provide many opportunities to address motor skill development during aerobic fitness activities. Motor skill development through fitness activity is the perfect area for you to consider the abilities and limitations of all students. Some are high achievers, others are low achievers, and still others have physical or intellectual disabilities. Provide opportunities for all students to develop physical skills and be successful in your classroom. If a student is severely disabled, you may need to contact someone who specializes in adapted physical education for assistance in developing an individualized education plan.

As adolescents become more active you will want to provide information to reduce the risk of injury or illness that may lead to periods of inactivity. This is especially true when the student leaves your physical education program and continues to be active after school or in the community. Observe the following safety guidelines:

▨ Supervise the program closely and individualize the activity.

▨ Explain rules clearly and insist that students follow them

▨ Have students wear protective clothing and gear appropriate for the sport, including

  • proper shoes for the activity,

  • helmets for cycling and other sports, and

  • light clothing in the heat.

- Obtain medical information concerning preexisting conditions.
- Minimize exposure to the sun and heat by using shaded space or by having students wear sunscreen and hats.
- Recognize that exercise or activity on very hot and humid days or very cold days may increase health risks. Young people have low tolerance to exercise under these conditions (Bar-Or and Malina 1995) because they
  - have a large surface area per unit of mass,
  - sweat at a lower rate,
  - have high metabolic heat production, and
  - take longer to acclimate to hot environments.
- Recognize signs and symptoms of heat illness or cold injury and do what you can to lessen the health risk.
  - Provide plenty of cool water, shade, and rest periods, and reduce intensity of activity.
  - Have students wear layered clothing and limit exposure to cold.
  - When necessary, conduct class indoors to limit exposure to air pollution.

Note: The above discussion of young people's environmental tolerance applies primarily to the prepubescent student and to a lesser extent with pubescent and postpubescent students.

Physical Best provides you and your students with the knowledge, skills, values, and confidence to engage in physical activity now and in the future through enjoyable activities.

Activities

Chapter 3 Activities Grid

Activity number	Activity title	Activity page	Concept	Middle school	High school	Reproducible (on CD-Rom)
3.1	Aerobic Capture	23	Definition	●		None
3.2	Clean Out Your Arteries	26	Health benefits	●		None
3.3	Aerobic Benefit Hunt	28	Health benefits	●		Aerobic Benefit Cards
						Aerobic Benefit Student Worksheet
3.4	Wanderer	30	Warm-up and cool-down; intensity	●		Heart Rate Record Sheet
3.5	Four-Corner Heart Healthy Warm-Up and Cool-Down	33	Warm-up and cool-down		●	Benefits of Warming Up and Cooling Down Poster
						Four-Corner Heart Healthy Warm-Up and Cool-Down Cards
3.6	Fitting in Fitness	36	Frequency	●		Basketball Handout
						Jogging Handout
						Tennis Handout
						Aerobics Handout
						Football Handout
						Volleyball Handout
						Skating Handout
						Hockey Handout
3.7	Heartbeat Stations	40	Intensity and time	●		Heartbeat Stations Score Sheet
3.8	Cross-Training Trio	42	Time and type	●	●	Aerobic Fitness: Cross-Training Activities Log
						Aerobic Fitness: Cross-Training Benefits and Guidelines
3.9	Target Zone Aerobic Martial Arts	45	Intensity and time		●	Target Zone Aerobic Martial Arts Recording Form
3.10	Continuous Relay	48	Intensity and time		●	Individual Workout Log

3.1 Aerobic Capture

MIDDLE SCHOOL

Aerobic fitness is the "ability to perform large muscle, dynamic, moderate to high intensity exercise for prolonged periods" (ACSM 2000, p. 68). Aerobic activity can help to reduce the build-up of fat deposits in the arteries, promoting a healthy cardiovascular system and reducing the risk of cardiovascular disease.

PURPOSE

- Students will be able to explain how the heart, lungs, vascular system, and muscles work together to send oxygen and nutrients throughout the body and to remove carbon dioxide from the body.
- Students will learn that aerobic fitness helps ensure that the cells of the body get the nutrients they need and are able to dispose of wastes.

RELATIONSHIP TO NATIONAL STANDARDS

Physical Education Standard 4: Achieves and maintains a health-enhancing level of physical fitness.

Physical Education Standard 5: Exhibits responsible personal and social behavior that respects self and others in physical activity settings.

Health Education Standard 1: Student will comprehend concepts related to health promotion and disease prevention.

EQUIPMENT

- 24 balls—six each of four different colors (Using balls of different sizes and shapes or different objects can add to the fun!)
- 4 trash bins
- 12 hula hoops
- 4 large cones
- Optional: 4 sets of different-colored shirts or pinnies to designate the members of the four different teams.

Reproducible

- none

PROCEDURE

1. Divide the playing area into four quadrants (see diagram). In the center of each quadrant, set a trash bin behind three hula hoops. In each trash bin place a white ball or any object that you want to have represent carbon dioxide. Place one ball that is assigned to each of the three opposing teams in each hula hoop, as described in step 5.

2. In each far corner of the playing area, behind the trash bin, place a large cone. This cone is the "Try Again" holding area.

3. Review the concept of aerobic fitness. Talk about the relationship among the heart, lungs, and vascular system when it comes to transporting oxygen throughout the body. Identify some of the other elements that are transported by the blood besides oxygen (vitamins, minerals, water, sugar, fat, electrolytes, triglycerides,

cholesterol, white blood cells, antibodies). Recall that carbon dioxide is one item that must be transported out of the body. Remind your students that using their muscles to stay physically active will help maintain and improve aerobic fitness.

4. Inform the students that each ball color represents a different item that the blood transports. Tell them what each color symbolizes. For example, blue can represent oxygen, green can represent vitamins, pink can represent sugar, and so on.

5. Divide the class into four teams that represent the heart, lungs, blood vessels, and muscles. Each team will guard one quadrant. If possible, use different-colored shirts or pinnies to identify each team. Also assign each team a colored ball to capture. For example, if you assign the heart team to capture oxygen, they must capture all three of the blue colored balls from the opposing teams' hoops.

6. The object of the game is for players to capture all three of their assigned item from the other three teams and place them in their own hoops, and to remove their carbon dioxide and put it in an opposing team's trash bin.

- Team members may throw the ball to another team member once and only if the receiver is within the same quadrant as the thrower.
- Players may tag opponents only when they are in their own quadrant.
- If tagged, players must go to the "Try Again" holding area in the capturing team's quadrant. The tagged players are free to go when a member of their team runs on the outside of the playing area and tags the captured person. Before they can rejoin the playing action, both team members must return to their quadrant by running on the outside of the playing area.

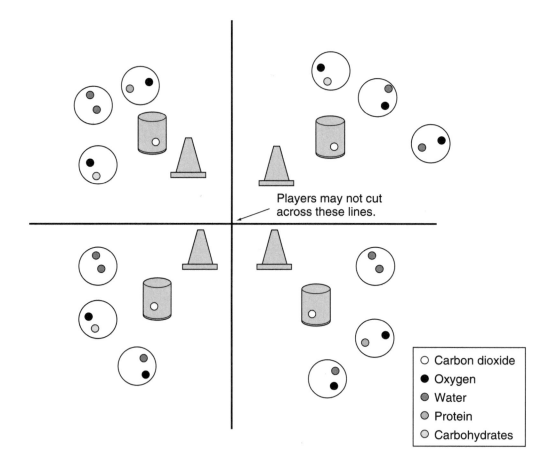

Players may not cut across these lines.

○ Carbon dioxide
● Oxygen
● Water
○ Protein
○ Carbohydrates

7. The first team to remove their carbon dioxide and to get all three of their designated colored balls in their hula hoops yells, "Stop." The team receives one point.

8. All balls from every team are returned to their original positions in the hula hoops and trash bins, and the game begins again. At this time you can change what the balls represent, to include all of the items carried by the blood. For example, for the game in the set-up diagram we included carbon dioxide, oxygen, water, protein, and carbohydrates. In the next game, you could include vitamins, sugar, minerals, and triglycerides.

TEACHING HINTS

▨ Remind the students that they must be alert as to personal and general space because so many students are moving in different directions at the same time.

▨ Remind students to tag one another gently.

▨ Keep students honest by ensuring that they run on the outside of the playing area when returning from being caught.

SAMPLE INCLUSION TIPS

▨ For a student with cerebral palsy, utilize balls with Velcro and a catcher's mitt or pad with Velcro to ensure success with catching the ball. After the student with a disability has caught the ball, allow him to throw the ball in his own manner. If the student with a disability cannot throw the ball, a peer could assist by throwing the ball for him. Other peers may use the same ball with or without the mitt.

▨ For classes that have students who might find the instructions difficult to follow, pair up team members the first time the activity is performed.

ASSESSMENT

At the end of class ask the teams (heart, lungs, blood vessels, and muscles) to discuss why their team is important to aerobic fitness. Ask each team what item it had to retrieve and what would happen if part of the body didn't get that item from the bloodstream.

Clean Out Your Arteries

MIDDLE SCHOOL

Health benefits—You can benefit in many ways from regular physical activity. Aerobic activity can help to reduce the build-up of fat deposits in the arteries, promoting a healthy cardiovascular system and reducing the risk of cardiovascular disease.

PURPOSE

Students will develop an understanding of the relationship between physical activity and cardiovascular health.

RELATIONSHIP TO NATIONAL STANDARDS

Physical Education Standard 4: Achieves and maintains a health-enhancing level of physical fitness.

Health Education Standard 1: Students will comprehend concepts related to health promotion and disease prevention.

Health Education Standard 3: Students will demonstrate the ability to practice health-enhancing behaviors and reduce health risks.

EQUIPMENT

- 4 hoops
- 8 cones
- 40 beanbags
- Student journals (if using second "Assessment" tip)

Reproducible

- none

PROCEDURE

1. Divide the activity space into four quadrants. Place one hoop and two cones in each quadrant (see diagram), and place 10 beanbags in each hoop.

2. Divide the class into four teams. Students on team A will compete against team B. Students on team C will compete against team D. Assign each team to a quadrant, and have teams play across (not diagonally) from each other.

3. Explain that each hoop represents an artery and each beanbag represents fat. The object of the game is to clean the fat out of their team's artery through physical activity.

4. On the whistle, direct students to run from their positions, as shown in the diagram, to their artery (hoop) and pick up a fat (beanbag), run the fat (beanbag) to the opposing team's quadrant, and place the fat (beanbag) in the opposing team's artery (hoop). Students must run clockwise around the perimeter of the activity space (half of the gym is best if possible, for safety reasons), on the outside of the cones before they remove a new beanbag from their hoop.

5. After three to five minutes, stop and count beanbags to see which team has the least amount of fat. The team that performed the most work will end up with the least amount of fat (beanbags) in their artery. Remind students that physical activity helps keep their arteries clear of fat deposits, and that benefit may increase with increased physical activity.

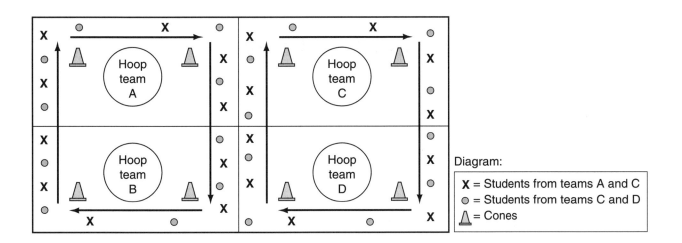

Diagram:

X = Students from teams A and C
⊙ = Students from teams C and D
△ = Cones

6. Redivide the fat (beanbags) evenly, and repeat the activity with the goal of each team reducing more fat than in the previous round. This might be a good time to alter team make-up, especially if students with disabilities are participating in the activity.

TEACHING HINTS

■ Make the activity sport-specific. As an alternative to using beanbags, use basketballs for fat and carts for arteries. Students dribble the balls to the opposing cart. Other options include practicing cradling for lacrosse or dribbling for soccer.

■ Students may carry only one object at a time.

■ Students must place, not throw, the objects into the hoop.

■ Students must move in the same direction (clockwise) at all times to avoid collisions.

SAMPLE INCLUSION TIPS

■ Students using wheelchairs can cut across the middle of the playing area instead of having to move around the cones at the perimeter.

■ Establish an area in the center of the playing area so the student using a wheelchair could wheel to that alternative space.

ASSESSMENT

■ Ask the students why one artery would end up with more fat than the other artery. Help them compare this to what actually may happen in the human body.

■ Have students journal five specific activities that would improve their cardiovascular system.

3.3 Aerobic Benefit Hunt

MIDDLE SCHOOL

Health benefits—Regular physical activity, especially aerobic fitness activities, has been proven to provide a wide array of health benefits.

PURPOSE

- Students will be able to identify the benefits of aerobic fitness.
- Through participation in various aerobic activities, students will be able to recognize activities that enhance aerobic fitness.

RELATIONSHIP TO NATIONAL STANDARDS

Physical Education Standard 3: Participates regularly in physical activity.

Physical Education Standard 4: Achieves and maintains a health-enhancing level of physical fitness.

Health Education Standard 1: Student will comprehend concepts related to health promotion and disease prevention.

EQUIPMENT

- Music and player
- Pencil or colored marker for each group

PROCEDURE

1. Organize students into groups of three or four.
2. Give each group a worksheet and a pencil or marker.
3. Place the Aerobic Benefit Cards on the floor, numbered side up, and scattered randomly throughout the playing area.

Reproducibles

- Aerobic Benefit Cards (Copy cards with provided benefits and aerobic activities or use your own benefits and activities.)
- Aerobic Benefit Student Worksheet, one for every three or four students

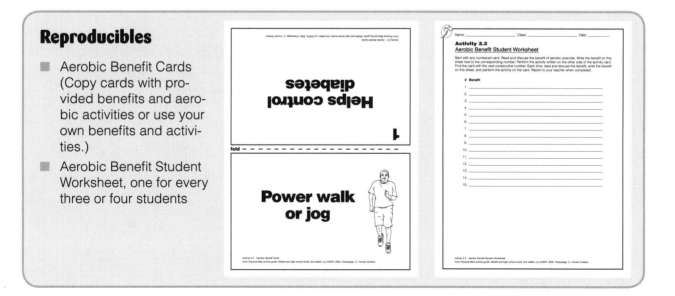

© Human Kinetics

4. When the music starts, each group goes to any card they wish. They must read the aerobic benefit, and write the benefit on their worksheet.

5. They must then turn the card over and read the aerobic activity. All group members must perform the activity together.

6. When the group has completed the aerobic activity for a predetermined amount of time, they must find the card with the *next consecutive number.* For example, if they started at card #8, they must find card #9, write the benefit on their worksheet, and perform the aerobic activity written on the other side of the card.

7. Continue until students have completed a predetermined number of cards, or continue for a certain length of time.

8. Bring students together to discuss
   • the benefits of aerobic activity that they have written on their worksheet (point out that doing aerobic fitness activities will help them stay healthy),
   • elements the activities have in common to identify how to determine whether an activity is aerobic, and
   • what aerobic activities students can do throughout a day.

TEACHING HINTS

▪ Determine the amount of time or repetitions for each card based on the intensity of the activity as well as the age and fitness level of the students.

▪ Present aerobic activities that may be new to your students or your locale, or ones in which few students have the opportunity to participate on their own.

SAMPLE INCLUSION TIPS

▪ For students with intellectual disabilities, use both verbal and visual aids/picture cues.

▪ Allow students with disabilities to attempt to perform activities prior to incorporating modifications.

ASSESSMENT

▪ Check worksheets for correct aerobic benefits.

▪ Have students turn to a neighbor and tell them three benefits of aerobic activity.

▪ Prepare a sheet of pictures that depict aerobic and nonaerobic activities. Ask students to identify the aerobic activities.

3.4 Wanderer

MIDDLE SCHOOL

A **warm-up** increases the temperature of the body and the elasticity of the muscles. A warm-up improves the muscles ability to perform work and reduces the risk of injury. A **cool-down** is the reverse process of the warm-up. A proper cool-down may reduce muscle soreness, help bring the body temperature back to normal ranges, and allow muscles to flush wastes generated by exercise. **Intensity** describes how hard a person exercises during a physical activity period. Optimal intensity depends on the age and fitness goals of the participant. Heart rate has traditionally been used as a measure of training intensity to develop aerobic fitness.

PURPOSE

▨ Students will be able to explain the benefits of warming up and cooling down.

▨ Students will understand training intensity using heart rate measurements.

RELATIONSHIP TO NATIONAL STANDARDS

Physical Education Standard 1: Demonstrates competency in motor skills and movement patterns needed to perform a variety of physical activities.

Health Education Standard 1: Students will comprehend concepts related to health promotion and disease prevention.

Dance Education Standard 6: Make connections between dance and healthful living.

EQUIPMENT

▨ Music with a good beat—in 4/4 time, with 128 to 135 beats per minute—and player

▨ Method to take pulse (heart rate monitors, wall clock with second hand, stopwatch for teacher)

▨ Pencils, one per student (optional; need if using worksheet)

PROCEDURE

1. Have students take their heart rate before beginning the activity. Tell students to write their beginning heart rate on the Heart Rate Record Sheet. (See *Physical Education for Lifelong Fitness: The Physical Best Teacher's Guide, Second Edition*, chapter 5, for information on taking the pulse.)

Reproducible

▨ Heart Rate Record Sheet (optional), one per student

Name: _____ Class: _____ Date: _____

Activity 3.4
Heart Rate Record Sheet

Part 1: Record your heart rate when your teacher signals you to do so.

Warm-Up	Cool-Down
Beginning heart rate _____	Beginning heart rate _____
Round 1 heart rate _____	Round 1 heart rate _____
Round 2 heart rate _____	Round 2 heart rate _____
Round 3 heart rate _____	Round 3 heart rate _____
Round 4 heart rate _____	Round 4 heart rate _____

Part 2: Now look over the heart rates you have recorded and answer the following questions:

For the Warm-Up

1. Did your heart rate rise?

2. What other changes did you notice?

For the Cool-Down

1. Did your heart rate go down (decreasing intensity)?

2. What other changes did you notice?

Activity 3.4 Heart Rate Record Sheet
From Physical Best activity guide: Middle and high school levels, 2nd edition, by NASPE, 2005, Champaign, IL: Human Kinetics.

2. Have students perform the following steps:

Grapevine right—4 counts

Grapevine left—4 counts

2 step touches—4 counts

4 quick heels front (left, right, left, right)—4 counts

Walk forward right, left, right, left knee up and a hop turn to the right (1/4 turn or 90 degrees)—4 counts

Walk back left, right, left, right knee up—4 counts

Slide step side to side: right, left, right, left—8 counts

Begin again, facing the new side.

3. If you desire, you can have students take and record their heart rate after each round. After four rounds, students are again facing the side where they began.

4. Have students quickly take their pulse. Tell students to remember what their warm-up heart rate is or to write it on the Heart Rate Record Sheet. Ask students whether their heart rate increased during the warm-up and by how much.

5. You can also use the activity as a cool-down: Have students take their heart rate after the active phase of the session. Then have students perform the Wanderer, decreasing the size (intensity) of their movements. After each round, have students take their heart rate and, if desired, record it on the Heart Rate Record Sheet. Their heart rate should decrease as the cool-down progresses.

TEACHING HINTS

- Teach one section of the grapevine at a time. Then work through the dance without music, turning to all four walls. Finally, add music.

- This dance can be used frequently as a class warm-up or cool-down. Once the students have mastered it, try having them do all of the steps to the left instead of to the right. For warm-up, increase the speed after four rounds (when students are back facing front). You can ask students to increase the size (intensity) of their movements. For a cool-down, do the reverse—ask students to decrease the size (intensity) of their movements.

- For another variation, divide students into four groups, and ask each group to make up an eight-count phrase of steps. Have groups demonstrate and teach their phrases to the class, then put the phrases together for a new warm-up.

- As an extension of this activity, have students check their heart rate during the main lesson activity as well.

SAMPLE INCLUSION TIPS

- Provide easier variations of the activities as needed (variation example: instead of a grapevine, two steps to the side).

- Students with disabilities or attention difficulties should be placed in front of class (groups/lines) to best focus on the directions and movements demonstrated.

- To assist students with diagnosed or undiagnosed learning disabilities, partner students to answer the questions on the optional worksheet.

ASSESSMENT

- Ask students to recall their heart rate after each of the four rounds. Discuss the questions on part 2 of the Heart Rate Record Sheet as a class (students may notice changes in heart rate, breathing rate, body temperature, and so on).
- Require students to fill out the Heart Rate Record Sheet for you to collect.

3.5 Four-Corner Heart Healthy Warm-Up and Cool-Down

HIGH SCHOOL

A **warm-up** increases the temperature of the body and the elasticity of the muscles. A warm-up improves the muscles' ability to perform work and reduces the risk of injury. A **cool-down** is the reverse process of the warm-up. A proper cool-down may reduce muscle soreness, help bring the body temperature back to normal ranges, and allow muscles to flush wastes generated by exercise.

PURPOSE

- Students will be able to explain the benefits of warming up and cooling down.
- Students will be able to describe the appropriate sequence of a warm-up and cool-down.

RELATIONSHIP TO NATIONAL STANDARDS

Health Education Standard 1: Students will comprehend concepts related to health promotion and disease prevention.

Health Education Standard 3: Students will demonstrate the ability to practice health-enhancing behaviors and reduce health risks.

EQUIPMENT

- Music—30-second segments with 10 seconds of no music between each segment—and player. (You'll need eight 30/10 segments for moderate warm-up and eight 30/10 segments for stretching.)
- One 4-inch strip of modeling clay

Reproducibles

- Benefits of Warming Up and Cooling Down Poster
- Four-Corner Heart Healthy Warm-Up and Cool-Down Cards

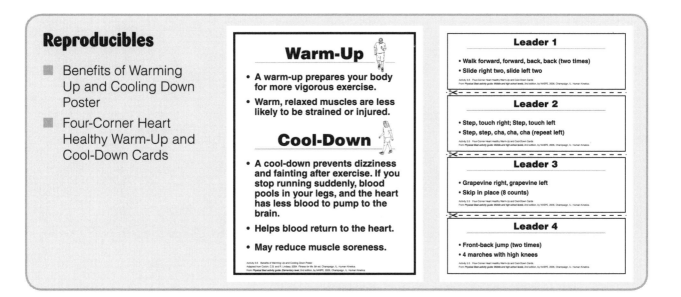

PROCEDURE

1. Hang a Benefits of Warming Up and Cooling Down Poster on the middle of each of the four walls of the activity area.

2. Explain the purpose of a warm-up. Reinforce the importance of warming up by explaining an analogy between muscles and modeling clay. Take a cold piece of modeling clay and try to stretch it; it will snap in two. Then take the same clay and work it in your hands until it is warm and very pliable. Stretch the "warmed" clay. Ask students to describe the difference in the two demonstrations. Ask students what could happen to bodies if they do not properly warm up (they should relate this to the "cold" clay).

   • Describe the two phases of a warm-up: physical activity and stretching. Emphasize that the two phases of a warm-up work together to prepare the body for more vigorous activity and to loosen and relax the muscles.

   • Explain that the goal of this activity is to gradually increase the heart rate and to help students understand how warming up can prevent injury. (If you're using this as a cool-down, explain that the goal of this activity is to gradually decrease the heart rate and to help students understand that cooling down brings the body temperature back to normal ranges and can reduce muscle soreness.)

3. Select four students to lead the activity. Give each leader a Four-Corner Heart Healthy Warm-Up and Cool-Down Card that states which activity the student will lead for 30 seconds.

4. Have each of the four leaders stand to the right of each Benefits Poster. Arrange other students in lines, facing Leader 1 (see diagram). Encourage students to read the Benefits Posters during their activity.

5. As the music begins, Leader 1 starts walking in place, which signals students to begin doing the same.

6. At the end of the first 30 seconds of music, the students jog slowly in place as they turn one-quarter turn to the right to face Leader 2. Students continue to jog in place until Leader 2 begins his or her activity. All students (including all of the leaders) follow Leader 2.

7. After 30 seconds, all students jog in place as they turn one-quarter turn to the right to face Leader 3. The same process is followed for Leader 4.

Leader 3

X	X	X	X	X
X	X	X	X	X

Leader 2   X   X   X   X   X   **Leader 4**

X	X	X	X	X
X	X	X	X	X

Leader 1

8. Once students return to face Leader 1, he or she begins the second movement written on his or her index card.

9. After the second complete rotation through all four Leaders, students are ready to begin the next phase of the warm-up: slow muscle stretching.

10. Follow the same four-corner process for the slow muscle stretching. This time each of the four leaders stretches a different part of the body. During the slow stretches, call on students to state a benefit of warming up or cooling down.

11. To use the same activity as a cool-down, follow the same procedures but reverse the order of the cards so that the most intense exercise (front-back jump) is done first and the least intense exercise (walking in place) is done last. Have students notice the differences in their bodies that result from the cool-down, and tell students that cooling down properly will reduce muscle soreness.

TEACHING HINTS

▓ Laminate the Benefits of Warming Up and Cooling Down Posters to preserve them for many years.

▓ Select a variety of students to serve as leaders of this activity.

SAMPLE INCLUSION TIPS

▓ Allow students with physical disabilities to adapt the movements. For example, instead of jogging, a student with movement disabilities might march.

▓ When given the opportunity to be a leader, allow students with speech difficulties to give a demonstration of the movement/activity while a peer or the teacher provides the voicing.

▓ For students with hearing impairments, match with hearing peers to assist with transition/movement to next station. While using music, place speakers on side and lower to floor to create vibrations from the rhythm/beat that a student with a hearing loss may recognize. Stopping the beat may provide cue to move to next station.

ASSESSMENT

▓ Ask students what changes they observed in their bodies as they warmed up or cooled down. Ask students why these changes are important (how do they help us).

▓ Have students design a poster or power point presentation that visually presents facts about and the benefits of warming up and cooling down.

3.6 Fitting in Fitness

MIDDLE SCHOOL

Frequency describes how often a person performs the targeted health-related physical activity. The minimum frequency for aerobic fitness activities is three days per week, while five to seven days is optimal.

PURPOSE

- Students will understand the importance of staying active most days of the week and will be encouraged to track their activity levels.
- Students will recognize physical activities that are aerobic (with oxygen) and anaerobic (without oxygen).
- Students will identify strategies that facilitate an active lifestyle.

RELATIONSHIP TO NATIONAL STANDARDS

Physical Education Standard 1: Demonstrates competency in motor skills and movement patterns needed to perform a variety of physical activities.

Physical Education Standard 3: Participates regularly in physical activity.

Physical Education Standard 4: Achieves and maintains a health-enhancing level of physical fitness.

Health Education Standard 1: Students will comprehend concepts related to health promotion and disease prevention.

Health Education Standard 3: Students will demonstrate the ability to practice health-enhancing behaviors and reduce health risks.

EQUIPMENT

The activities that you choose and the space that you have will dictate the equipment needed. Following are some examples of equipment needed for some of the activities described in the procedure.

- 1 to 6 basketballs
- 1 to 3 footballs
- 1 to 6 volleyballs
- 4 to 6 tennis rackets and balls
- 4 to 6 steps (for step aerobics)
- 4 to 6 hockey sticks and 2 hockey pucks or balls
- Music and player

Reproducibles

Note: These Fitting in Fitness handouts are only a sampling of some of the activities students might like to participate in outside of class. You can design additional handouts tailored to your students' needs.

- ▓ Basketball Handout (shown here as example)
- ▓ Jogging Handout (shown here as example)
- ▓ Tennis Handout (shown here as example)
- ▓ Aerobics Handout
- ▓ Football Handout
- ▓ Volleyball Handout
- ▓ Skating Handout
- ▓ Hockey Handout

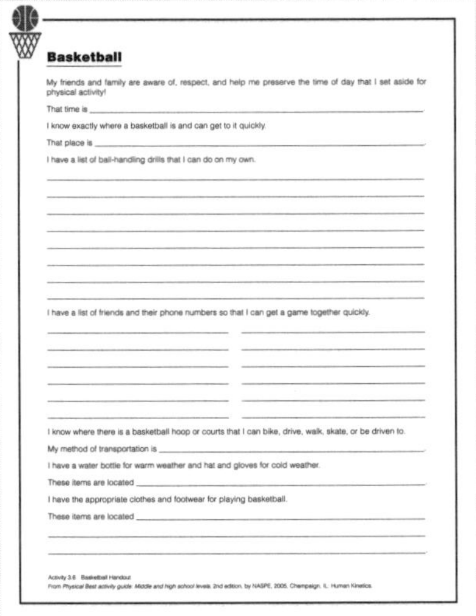

Basketball

My friends and family are aware of, respect, and help me preserve the time of day that I set aside for physical activity!

That time is _____

I know exactly where a basketball is and can get to it quickly.

That place is _____

I have a list of ball-handling drills that I can do on my own.

_____
_____
_____
_____
_____
_____

I have a list of friends and their phone numbers so that I can get a game together quickly.

_____ _____
_____ _____
_____ _____

I know where there is a basketball hoop or courts that I can bike, drive, walk, skate, or be driven to.

My method of transportation is _____

I have a water bottle for warm weather and hat and gloves for cold weather.

These items are located _____

I have the appropriate clothes and footwear for playing basketball.

These items are located _____

Activity 3.6 Basketball Handout
From Physical Best activity guide: Middle and high school levels, 2nd edition, by NASPE, 2005, Champaign, IL: Human Kinetics.

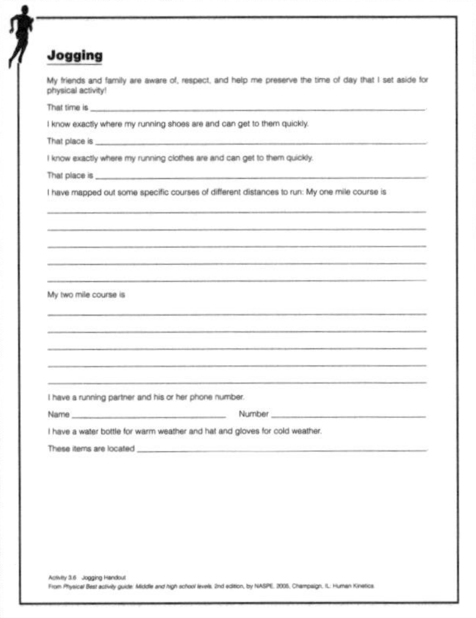

Jogging

My friends and family are aware of, respect, and help me preserve the time of day that I set aside for physical activity!

That time is _____

I know exactly where my running shoes are and can get to them quickly.

That place is _____

I know exactly where my running clothes are and can get to them quickly.

That place is _____

I have mapped out some specific courses of different distances to run: My one mile course is

_____
_____
_____
_____

My two mile course is

_____
_____
_____
_____
_____

I have a running partner and his or her phone number.

Name _____ Number _____

I have a water bottle for warm weather and hat and gloves for cold weather.

These items are located _____

Activity 3.6 Jogging Handout
From Physical Best activity guide: Middle and high school levels, 2nd edition, by NASPE, 2005, Champaign, IL: Human Kinetics.

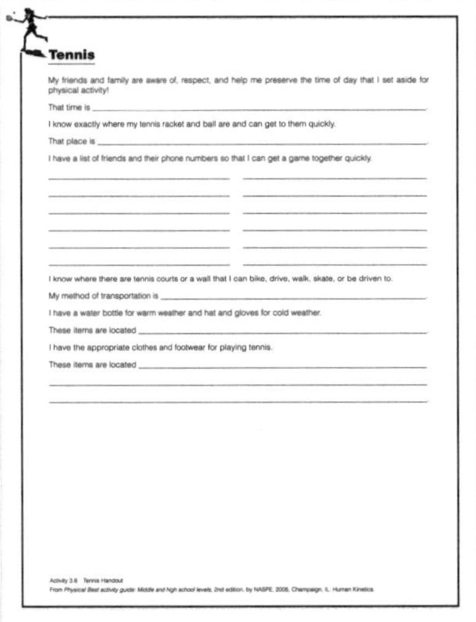

Tennis

My friends and family are aware of, respect, and help me preserve the time of day that I set aside for physical activity!

That time is _____

I know exactly where my tennis racket and ball are and can get to them quickly.

That place is _____

I have a list of friends and their phone numbers so that I can get a game together quickly.

_____ _____
_____ _____
_____ _____
_____ _____

I know where there are tennis courts or a wall that I can bike, drive, walk, skate, or be driven to.

My method of transportation is _____

I have a water bottle for warm weather and hat and gloves for cold weather.

These items are located _____

I have the appropriate clothes and footwear for playing tennis.

These items are located _____

Activity 3.6 Tennis Handout
From Physical Best activity guide: Middle and high school levels, 2nd edition, by NASPE, 2005, Champaign, IL: Human Kinetics.

PROCEDURE

1. Set up seven stations indoors or outdoors that will help your students to participate in seven different activities (e.g., basketball, volleyball, jogging, walking, Frisbee, football, soccer, dance, hockey, or aerobic dance). Include activities that are more aerobic (moderate intensity) and more anaerobic (vigorous intensity) in nature. Set up stations that appeal to your students and that represent activities that they most enjoy participating in both in physical education class and outside of class. Number the stations 1 to 7.

2. Remind the class that the Surgeon General suggests people should participate in physical activity most days of the week. Remind them that the time they spend in an activity and the intensity of the workout can affect how often they exercise.

3. Explain to the class that aerobic activities are activities in which their muscles require oxygen to produce energy. Tell students that in aerobic activities, they are active for a long period of time and can tell that their heart and lungs are working. Walking, biking, and jogging down the soccer field are aerobic activities. Explain

that aerobic activities should be done on most or all days of the week. But there is also another type of activity that is good for you. Anaerobic activities often are done for very short periods of time and use muscles in a more intense way. Think of sprinting or lifting a weight. Anaerobic physical activity is done in short, fast bursts in which the heart cannot supply blood and oxygen as fast as muscles use it (Corbin 2004).

© Human Kinetics

4. Tell the students that the seven stations that they will be moving through represent the seven days of the week. Ask the students what some of the reasons might be for taking a day off (e.g., to let your body recover after more intense, anaerobic activity). Inform them that in this activity they will be reviewing strategies to help them to stay active on most days of the week.

5. Describe to the class what activity they will be doing at each station. Examples:

- Basketball—Students could play one-on-one, two-on-two, or three-on-three; depending on the number of students who are at a station. They could practice running lay-ups, dribble in and out of cones, side shuffle as they pass, practice ball-handling drills, and so forth.

- Jogging—Students could run in pairs on a designated path or anywhere in sight of the teacher.

- Volleyball—Students could play two-on-two, or they could practice sets, forearm passes (to themselves, in pairs, with the group, or against a wall), and vertical jumps.

6. Divide the class into pairs. Tell the pairs of students to go to a station. Each station should be limited to three pairs.

7. Start the music.

8. Allow students to participate in an activity at their stations until the music stops at a predetermined time. Students at more intense (anaerobic) stations may need to take active rests (such as marching in place).

9. When the music stops, students rotate to the next station and then stretch.

10. When the music starts again, students should begin the new activity.

TEACHING HINTS

■ By changing the activities at each station, you can reinforce the idea that there are many types of physical activities for students to choose from.

- Use the sport-specific handouts (on the CD-ROM) to start your students thinking about the strategies for staying active outside of class. The handouts can be filled in for homework.

SAMPLE INCLUSION TIP

If you have students with physical disabilities, work with an adapted P.E. specialist to adapt activities for each station.

ASSESSMENT

- Conduct a question-and-answer session. Ask questions such as the following: What makes an activity aerobic? What activities were aerobic? What makes an activity anaerobic? What activities were anaerobic? What activities would be the easiest to participate in outside of class? What strategies for staying active were the most important to you and why?

- Have students track their activity levels. They can develop their own method to track their activity frequency, intensity, time, and type by creating logs on paper or by generating a graph or calendar on the computer. Students can also use the "Presidential Youth Active Lifestyle log" (www.presidentschallenge.org) or other online fitness logs available to youth.

3.7 Heartbeat Stations

MIDDLE SCHOOL

Intensity is the level at which you perform an activity. Intensity for aerobic activity can be correlated with heart rate, and can affect the **time** in which you participate in the activity. For example, if you choose to jog at the upper limits of your target heart rate range (THR), a higher intensity at 80 percent of your maximum heart rate (MHR), you will not be able to jog as long as you would if you worked at the lower range of your THR (60 percent of MHR).

PURPOSE

Students will participate in a variety of activities to understand how physical activity at varying intensity levels influences their heart rate, perceived exertion, and amount of time they will be able to maintain the activity.

RELATIONSHIP TO NATIONAL STANDARDS

Physical Education Standard 1: Demonstrates competency in motor skills and movement patterns needed to perform a variety of physical activities.

Physical Education Standard 4: Achieves and maintains a health-enhancing level of physical fitness.

Health Education Standard 3: Student demonstrates the ability to practice health-enhancing behaviors and reduce health risks.

EQUIPMENT

- Heart rate monitors (if available) or a wall clock with a second hand
- Pencils, one per student
- Stopwatch

PROCEDURE

1. Define intensity. Ask students to predict which aerobic fitness activities have greater intensity.

2. As a warm-up, have students consecutively participate in four activities—walking, power walking, jogging, and sprinting—for 1 minute each, with an active rest (such as marching in place) for 15 seconds between activities.

3. Set up an aerobic fitness circuit with activities that vary in intensity: walking through cones, jumping rope, jogging around the gym, dribbling a soccer ball, running an agility ladder, and so on.

4. Divide students into groups, and assign each group a station.

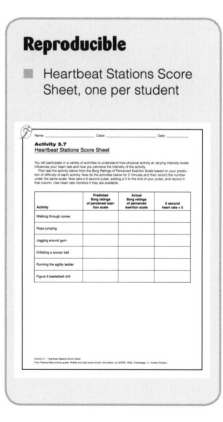

Reproducible

- Heartbeat Stations Score Sheet, one per student

40

5. Upon completing each station, have students measure their heart rate, either with the heart rate monitors or by counting their pulse for six seconds and adding zero to the number. Have students record their heart rate and their Borg Perceived Exertion Rating on the Heartbeat Stations Score Sheet.

6. Continue to rotate students through the stations until all stations are completed.

TEACHING HINTS

As a variation, ask each group to develop a station and teach it to the class.

SAMPLE INCLUSION TIP

For students with physical disabilities, supply or work with a P.E. specialist to develop an alternate, adapted activity at each station.

ASSESSMENT

- Have each student explain which of their predictions of intensity at the start of the activity were correct and why.

- Ask students to identify the station at which their hearts beat the fastest and slowest and at which they had the highest and lowest perceived exertion and explain why.

- Ask students how their activity time might be affected at these stations.

Borg Rating of Perceived Exertion Scale

6	No exertion at all
7	
8	Extremely light
9	Very light
10	
11	Light
12	
13	Somewhat hard
14	
15	Hard (heavy)
16	
17	Very hard
18	
19	Extremely hard
20	Maximal exertion

Borg RPE Scale © Gunnar Borg, 1970, 1985, 1994, 1998.

Reprinted, by permission, from G. Borg, 1998, *Borg's perceived exertion and pain scales* (Champaign, IL: Human Kinetics), 47.

3.8

Cross-Training Trio

MIDDLE AND HIGH SCHOOL

Time is how long you exercise during one bout of exercise. **Type** is the kind of exercise you engage in.

PURPOSE

Through in-class discussion and a homework assignment:

- Students will understand and apply the time component of the FITT Guidelines.
- Students will understand and apply the type component of the FITT Guidelines.
- Students will learn or review safety guidelines for participation in an aerobic fitness activity.

RELATIONSHIP TO NATIONAL STANDARDS

Physical Education Standard 1: Demonstrates competency in motor skills and movement patterns needed to perform a variety of physical activities.

Physical Education Standard 3: Participates regularly in physical activity.

Physical Education Standard 4: Achieves and maintains a health-enhancing level of physical fitness.

Health Education Standard 1: Students will comprehend concepts related to health promotion and disease prevention.

Health Education Standard 3: Students will demonstrate the ability to practice health-enhancing behaviors and reduce health risks.

EQUIPMENT

Activity will be done on student time and equipment is determined by student activity selection.

Reproducibles

- Aerobic Fitness: Cross-Training Activities Log, one per student
- Aerobic Fitness: Cross-Training Benefits and Guidelines, one per student

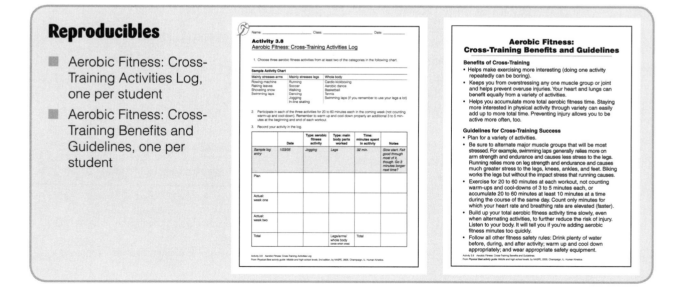

PROCEDURE

1. At the end of a class in which aerobic fitness was the focus, distribute one Aerobic Fitness: Cross-Training Benefits and Guidelines Sheet to each student.

2. Discuss the "Benefits of Cross-Training" section of the sheet. Discuss how the time component of FITT may be best addressed through varying activities. For example, a person is less likely to become bored or injured when alternating activities and muscle groups or joints stressed, thus allowing them to participate for an adequate duration to receive a health benefit.

3. Discuss the "Guidelines for Cross-Training Success" section of the sheet. Emphasize that the focus of this activity is to develop aerobic fitness, so the type component of the FITT principle will be important to address correctly.

4. Suggest the following cross-training plan for developing aerobic fitness: You jog home from school one day; you perform resistance training another day; and you in-line skate around your neighborhood a third day. Ask the following questions:

   • Does each activity help enhance aerobic fitness? (No, the weightlifting won't; we also don't know how long each aerobic activity lasts.)

   • Do the two aerobic fitness activities alternate major muscles and joints that they stress? (No, they both stress mainly the legs.)

5. Suggest the following cross-training plan for developing aerobic fitness: You bike home from school one day; this takes you 25 minutes. You swim laps for 10 minutes in addition to playing at the pool for 10 minutes on another day. You walk to the mall; this takes you 32 minutes. Ask the same questions as in step 4. The following is a sample answer: Yes, they are performed long enough (20 or more minutes total in the same day), are specific to aerobic fitness development (i.e., all three work the heart and lungs), and vary in muscles and joints stressed as well as vary in joint impact.

6. Distribute one Aerobic Fitness: Cross-Training Activities Log per student. Have individuals or partners create a cross-training plan that includes three activities that enhance aerobic fitness. Allow them to record their plan on the log. Have them ask themselves the same questions as in step 4.

7. Review and approve or edit student plans.

© Human Kinetics

8. Direct students to perform their plan in the coming two weeks, participating in each activity one time each week, and record their actual activity on the log.

9. Have students turn in their logs and paragraphs (see "Assessment" ideas).

TEACHING HINTS

▓ Be sure to monitor students' participation through logs and discussions to emphasize safe application of all training principles.

▓ Reinforce the "Guidelines for Cross-Training Success" as needed to ensure that students understand the concepts behind this approach.

▓ When revisiting this lesson, tie in the frequency component of FITT by having students plan one month of continued cross-training for aerobic fitness, using multiple (four or more) copies of the Aerobic Fitness: Cross-Training Activities Log form. Require variations from the original plan to determine whether students know how to safely apply what they've learned.

SAMPLE INCLUSION TIP

Work individually with students who need assistance in deciding the activities they will select for their cross-training plan, including modifications as needed.

ASSESSMENT

▓ Review or have partners review student logs to determine whether they understand how to apply the time and type components of the FITT Guidelines to aerobic fitness development through cross-training.

▓ Require each student to write a cohesive paragraph about how they may have benefited (or will benefit) from their cross-training experience. They should mention how they did (or may) increase total time working on aerobic fitness and how they addressed the type component of the FITT Guidelines.

3.9

Target Zone Aerobic Martial Arts (Cardio-Kickboxing)

HIGH SCHOOL

Intensity is the level at which you perform an activity, ranging from low to moderate to vigorous. To reach your target heart rate during exercise, it is recommended that you perform the activity to 60 to 85 percent of your maximal heart rate. The goal of an aerobic fitness training session is for students to exercise in their target heart rate zone for at least 20 minutes.

PURPOSE

- Students will learn to manipulate their intensity level in order to work in their aerobic target heart rate zone.

- Through recording their rating of perceived exertion, students will become aware of what it feels like to work in their target heart rate zone. They will also record the time spent in their target heart rate zone.

RELATIONSHIP TO NATIONAL STANDARDS

Physical Education Standard 1: Demonstrates competency in motor skills and movement patterns needed to perform a variety of physical activities.

Physical Education Standard 4: Achieves and maintains a health-enhancing level of physical fitness.

Health Education Standard 3: Students will demonstrate the ability to practice health-enhancing behaviors and reduce health risks.

EQUIPMENT

- Heart rate monitors (if available), wall clock with second hand, or stopwatch for the teacher
- Aerobic martial arts or cardio-kickboxing video
- VCR and television or DVD player and monitor
- Pencils, one per student

PROCEDURE

1. Before class, set up the video and television or DVD and monitor with an aerobic martial arts or cardio-kickboxing video.

2. Review what *intensity* means, and give or demonstrate examples of manipulating it (e.g., with low-impact or high-impact movements) to stay in the target heart rate zone. Review the Borg scale.

3. Have students put on heart rate monitors (if available).

Reproducible

- Target Zone Aerobic Martial Arts Recording Form

Name: _____ Class: _____ Date: _____

Activity 3.9
Target Zone Aerobic Martial Arts Recording Form

Activity	Time	Borg scale	6 sec heart rate
	10 min		
	20 min		
Activity	Time	Borg scale	6 sec heart rate
	10 min		
	20 min		
Activity	Time	Borg scale	6 sec heart rate
	10 min		
	20 min		
Activity	Time	Borg scale	6 sec heart rate
	10 min		
	20 min		
Activity	Time	Borg scale	6 sec heart rate
	10 min		
	20 min		
Activity	Time	Borg scale	6 sec heart rate
	10 min		
	20 min		
Activity	Time	Borg scale	6 sec heart rate
	10 min		
	20 min		
Activity	Time	Borg scale	6 sec heart rate
	10 min		
	20 min		
Activity	Time	Borg scale	6 sec heart rate
	10 min		
	20 min		

Activity 3.9 Target Zone Aerobic Martial Arts Recording Form
From *Physical Best activity guide: Middle and high school levels, 2nd edition,* by NASPE, 2005, Champaign, IL: Human Kinetics.

4. Ask students to take a resting heart rate (optional).

5. Ask students to recall what their target heart rate zone is, or provide an age-appropriate target heart rate zone for them. Tell them that their goal during this workout is to gradually work up to their target heart rate zone and then to try to stay in it for at least 20 minutes.

6. Review the basic moves presented in the video and have students practice them while providing cues about correct form. Then start the aerobic martial arts workout.

7. Midway through the workout, ask students to rate themselves on the Borg scale and to check their heart rate. Remind them to remember their ratings to record on the workout log once the session is complete. Have them adjust their movements to be more or less intense if they are below or above the target heart rate zone.

8. After the video is over, have students record heart rate and perceived exertion information on the Target Zone Aerobic Martial Arts Recording Form.

TEACHING HINTS

▨ Use a variety of previewed aerobic and cardio-kickboxing videos.

▨ Explain the value and purpose of using the Borg scale:

Perceived exertion is how hard you feel like your body is working. It is based on the physical sensations a person experiences during physical activity, including increased heart rate, increased respiration or breathing rate, increased sweating, and muscle fatigue. Although this is a subjective measure, a high correlation exists

© Human Kinetics

between a person's perceived exertion rating times 10 and the actual heart rate during physical activity; so a person's exertion rating may provide a fairly good estimate of the actual heart rate during activity (Borg 1998).

SAMPLE INCLUSION TIP

Place students with visual or auditory impairments close to the monitor. Pair them with buddies who will call out or sign movement directions.

ASSESSMENT

- Ask students to explain to you the principle of intensity and how it can be manipulated.

- To assess students' understanding of perceived exertion, have them describe what it feels like to be in their target heart rate zone. Ask, "How would you know if you were in your target heart rate zone without using a heart rate monitor?"

- Have students sign out a heart rate monitor and do a favorite sport or activity to see if the activity is aerobic in terms of intensity and time. Have them record their activity session on their workout log and comment as to what they discovered.

- The log has been designed with space for recording multiple workout sessions so that students can chart their progress over time. Students can store their workout logs in their portfolios or journals for future use and reference.

Borg Rating of Perceived Exertion Scale

6	No exertion at all
7	
8	Extremely light
9	Very light
10	
11	Light
12	
13	Somewhat hard
14	
15	Hard (heavy)
16	
17	Very hard
18	
19	Extremely hard
20	Maximal exertion

Borg RPE Scale © Gunnar Borg, 1970, 1985, 1994, 1998.

Reprinted, by permission, from G. Borg, 1998, *Borg's perceived exertion and pain scales* (Champaign, IL: Human Kinetics), 47.

3.10

Continuous Relay

HIGH SCHOOL

Intensity is the level at which an activity is performed, ranging from low to moderate to vigorous. To reach target heart rates during exercise, students have to elevate their heart rates to at least 60 percent of their maximal heart rate. The eventual goal of an aerobic fitness session is for students to exercise in their target heart rate zone for a minimum of 20 minutes. **Time** is the duration of activity. An increase in time can lead to improved fitness levels.

PURPOSE

- Students will elevate and maintain an appropriate exercise heart rate (60 to 85 percent max) during a continuous relay for a predetermined period of time.
- Students will be able to self-monitor their activity levels using beats-per-minute.
- Students will work to maintain or increase their fitness level as needed, with the goal of sustaining aerobic fitness activity for 20 minutes.

RELATIONSHIP TO NATIONAL STANDARDS

Physical Education Standard 4: Achieves and maintains a health-enhancing level of physical fitness.

Health Education Standard 1: Students will comprehend concepts related to health promotion and disease prevention.

Health Education Standard 3: Students will demonstrate the ability to practice health-enhancing behaviors and reduce health risks.

EQUIPMENT

- Appropriate fast-paced music and player
- Pencils, one per student
- Jump ropes (optional), enough for two-thirds of the class
- Pedometers (optional), one per student
- See "Teaching Hints" for other potential equipment needs

PROCEDURE

1. Introduce the activity by briefly discussing the importance of exercising in the appropriate target heart rate zone for developing aerobic fitness, what type of activities elevate heart rate, and what a lower resting heart rate may indicate.

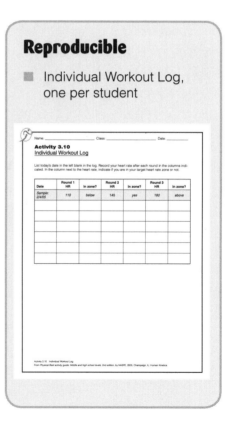

Reproducible

- Individual Workout Log, one per student

Name: _____ Class: _____ Date: _____

Activity 3.10
Individual Workout Log

List today's date in the left blank in the log. Record your heart rate after each round in the columns indicated. In the column next to the heart rate, indicate if you are in your target heart rate zone or not.

Date	Round 1 HR	In zone?	Round 2 HR	In zone?	Round 3 HR	In zone?
Sample: 2/4/05	110	below	145	yes	180	above

Activity 3.10 Individual Workout Log
From *Physical Best activity guide: Middle and high school levels*, 2nd edition, by NASPE. 2005, Champaign, IL: Human Kinetics.

2. Have students calculate their target heart rate zone (60 to 85 percent max), or provide these numbers for the age range in the class.

3. Direct students to take their heart rates before beginning the activity. You can use the Heart Rate Based on a 10-Second Count table to help students quickly compute their heart rates.

4. After an appropriate warm-up, divide students into groups of three. Student 1 is located on the end line of a basketball court. Student 2 is located on the center line. Student 3 is located on the other end line. If a lined court is not available, use another space marker such as cones.

5. Start the music.

6. End-line students perform rope-jumping skills (if no ropes—students can still perform the skills with an imaginary rope). The middle student is the runner. The student starts running toward one of the end-line students. Upon the runner's arrival, the jumper becomes the runner and heads toward the teammate located at the other end of the gym. Continue this activity for two to three minutes.

7. After one "round" lasting two to three minutes, stop the music and signal students to check their heart rates. Remind them to see if they are in their appropriate zone or if they need to increase or decrease their exercise intensity level. Have them fill in heart rate and zone on their recording log.

8. Start music and continue for another two to three minute "round."

9. Stop the music and direct students to check heart rates again. Have them record information on the log.

10. Continue for a predetermined period of time or number of rounds.

11. Close the activity by briefly reviewing the concepts taught in this activity.

TEACHING HINTS

▓ Total time of activity should be based upon fitness level of students. Schedule rest periods as needed.

▓ As a variation, give students on the center line a piece of sport equipment (e.g., a basketball) and have them perform a specific stationary ball skill (e.g., figure-eight passes at the knee), or perform muscular strength and endurance activities (e.g., variations of sit-ups or push-ups), before running to an end-line team member. Keep the number of repetitions low.

▓ For another variation, change activities at the end lines with each "round." Students can identify stationary activities that will increase or maintain an appropriate

Heart Rate Based on a 10-Second Count

Beats	Heart rate	Beats	Heart rate
10	60	22	132
11	66	23	138
12	72	24	144
13	78	25	150
14	84	26	156
15	90	27	162
16	96	28	168
17	102	29	174
18	108	30	180
19	114	31	186
20	120	32	192
21	126	33	198

exercise heart rate (e.g., line jumps, jumping jacks, or stretching, if the student needs to lower his or her heart rate).

■ For students who are new to using their target heart rate zones, display a large poster to help them check whether their heart rate is at an appropriate level such as a chart that offers the numbers for the age range in the class.

■ Have students use pedometers to keep track of how many steps they were able to attain and then add all three students' steps together. Remember that students' heights will affect their number of steps, so it's best not to compare the number of steps to other teams unless students are of similar height.

SAMPLE INCLUSION TIP

For students using wheelchairs, student may self-propel (wheel) from one end of the facility to the other and perform appropriate activities at the end line. Allow students using wheelchairs to substitute upper body arm movements for lower body leg movements.

ASSESSMENT

■ Have students tell their team members what their heart rate was at the beginning and end and discuss its meaning.

■ Review the logs students maintained during the activity. Save these for students to add to when revisiting this activity (you may want to avoid having students stop to record numbers too often—this defeats the purpose of keeping the heart rate elevated). Taking preexercise heart rate and postexercise heart rate is usually enough for a discussion.

■ If using pedometers, students can record both their individual and group scores to be compared when the activity is revisited in the future.

■ Gauge the amount of time the class or individual students can maintain the activity, as you revisit it, over a period of time.

■ Question students both orally and in writing about intensity, time, and how to adjust their heart rate and maintain it in the target heart rate zone. For example: If you want to participate in an activity for a long duration, what intensity should you work at? (low to moderate—toward the low end of the target heart rate zone).

CHAPTER

4

Muscular Strength and Endurance

Chapter Contents

- Defining Muscular Strength and Endurance

- Teaching Guidelines for Muscular Strength and Endurance

- Training Methods for Muscular Strength and Endurance

- Motor Skill Development Through Muscular Strength and Endurance Activities

- Activities

© Human Kinetics

Although the literature does not offer a clear-cut conclusion about whether adolescents attain health benefits from resistance training similar to those that adults achieve, middle and high school students can safely improve muscular strength and endurance if they follow appropriate training guidelines.

Sothern, Loftin, Suskind et al. (1999) reported findings that the prepubescent child is at increased risk for injury because of a reduction in joint flexibility caused by rapid growth of long bones. Their findings suggest that strength gains may reduce the risk of acute sports injuries and overuse injuries.

For more information concerning the principles of training for muscular strength and endurance, refer to *Physical Education for Lifelong Fitness: The Physical Best Teacher's Guide, Second Edition.*

This chapter includes several activities for developing muscular strength and endurance in middle and high school students.

Defining Muscular Strength and Endurance

Muscular strength is the ability of a muscle or muscle group to exert a maximal force against a resistance one time through the full range of motion. A student perceives this as the ability to act independently and lift and carry objects without assistance. *Muscular endurance* is the ability of a muscle or muscle group to exert a submaximal force repeatedly over a period of time.

Unlike activities conducted at the elementary level that focus on using the child's own body weight to build muscular strength and endurance, activities at the middle school and high school levels may involve lifting light weights (using machine weights and free weights) to build muscular strength and endurance. You will find the physiological responses to physical activity and exercise training are more similar to those of adults and that adult training methods are more applicable as adolescents progress from middle school to high school.

Potential benefits of resistance training include the following:

- Increased muscular strength (everyday activities become easier)
- Increased muscular endurance (able to participate in leisure activity without having sore or tired muscles)
- Improvement in aerobic fitness through muscular fitness circuit training (able to participate in leisure activities without getting tired)
- Prevention of musculoskeletal injury (will not get hurt as easily or often)
- Improved sports performance (become a better player)
- Reduced risk of fractures in adulthood (builds stronger bones)
- Exercise during the skeletal growth period is better for bone development, increasing bone strength and bone growth (builds stronger bones, reduced risk of osteoporosis)

Teaching Guidelines for Muscular Strength and Endurance

As with each area of health-related fitness, the principles of training (progression, overload, specificity, regularity, and individuality) should be incorporated into the activity. Manipulate the FITT Guidelines based on the age of each student. Keep in mind that chronological age may not match physiological maturation. The guidelines in table 4.1 are merely principles

TABLE 4.1 FITT Guidelines Applied to Muscular Fitness

Ages	9-11 years[a,b]	12-14 years[a,b]	15-16 years[a,b]	17+ years[c]
Frequency	2 or 3 days/wk	2 or 3 days/wk	2 or 3 days/wk	2 days/wk
Intensity	Very light weight	Light weight	Moderate weight	Light to heavy weight (based on type selected)
Time	At least 1 set (may do 2 sets), at least 20-30 min	At least 1 set (may do 3 sets), 6-15 reps, at least 20-30 min	At least 1 set (may do 3 or 4 sets), 6-15 reps, at least 20-30 min	Minimum 1 set, 8-12 reps
Type	Major muscle groups, 1 exercise/muscle or muscle group	Major muscle groups, 1 exercise/muscle or muscle group	Major muscle groups, 2 exercises/ muscle or muscle group	Major muscle groups, 8-10 exercises; select muscular strength, power, or endurance

[a]Modified from AAP (2001). "Strength training by children and adolescents (RE0048)". *Pediatrics*, 107(6): 1470-1472.

[b]Modified from Faigenbaum, A.D. et al. 1996. Youth resistance training: Position statement paper and literature review. *Strength and conditioning* 18(6): 62-75.

[c]Modified from American College of Sports Medicine. (2000). *ACSM's guidelines for exercise testing and prescription*, 6th ed. (Baltimore, MD: Lippincott, Williams, and Wilkins).

for the development of muscular strength and endurance. Kraemer and Fleck (1993) suggest the following guidelines for resistance exercise:

- For students 11 to 13 years of age, teach all basic exercise techniques; continue progressive loading of each exercise; emphasize exercise techniques; introduce more advanced exercises with little or no resistance.

- Students 14 years and older may begin basic resistance training emphasizing correct technique and progress to more advanced training techniques. Once they master technique, high school students may begin to participate in adult resistance training programs.

Training Methods for Muscular Strength and Endurance

A student with no resistance training experience should begin at the previous level, regardless of age, and move to the next level as he or she develops exercise tolerance, skill, and understanding of the lifting techniques.

Several recommendations or position stands exist for resistance training (not weight lifting; see chapter 6 in *Physical Education for Lifelong Fitness: The Physical Best Teacher's Guide, Second Edition*) providing guidance in developing adolescents' resistance training programs (ACSM 2000; AAP 2001; Hass et al. 2001; NSCS 1985). Save resistance training using machine weights or barbells for postpubescent students. Use the guidelines in table 4.1 to help you develop a safe and developmentally appropriate unit on muscular strength and endurance.

Motor Skill Development Through Muscular Strength and Endurance Activities

It is not always necessary, nor appropriate, to use the weight room to develop muscular strength and endurance. Students may engage in a variety of motor skills to increase muscular strength and endurance. For example, older students may enjoy team-building activities that require arm strength for success. Encourage middle school and high school students to select activities they enjoy now and will continue to participate in after graduation.

Motor skill development through fitness activity is the perfect area for you to consider the abilities and disabilities of all students. Some are high achievers, others are low achievers, and still others have physical or intellectual disabilities. Provide opportunities for all students to develop physical skills and be successful in your classroom. If a student has severe disabilities, you may need to contact someone who specializes in adapted physical education for assistance in developing an individualized education plan (IEP). Many of the Physical Best activities either incorporate a variety of motor skills or allow you to create modifications to the activity to address the motor development needs of your students.

Activities

Chapter 4 Activities Grid

Activity number	Activity title	Activity page	Concept	Middle school	High school	Reproducible (on CD-Rom)
4.1	Imposter—Or Not?	56	Definition	•		Imposter—Or Not? Station Task Cards
						Imposter—Or Not? Worksheet
4.2	Go for the Team Gold	59	Health benefits	•		Go for the Team Gold Task Cards
						Go for the Team Gold Handout
4.3	Safely Finding the 8- to 12-Rep Range	61	Intensity		•	Weight-Training Chart
4.4	Rev-Up Roulette	64	Warm-up and cool-down	•		Rev-Up Roulette Warm-Up Spinner
						Rev-Up Roulette Cool-Down Spinner
4.5	Warm Up With Weights	67	Warm-up and cool-down		•	Weight-Training Chart
4.6	Muscles in Action	69	Specificity	•		Muscles in Action Exercise Posters
						Muscle Cards
						Labeled Muscle Diagram
						Muscles in Action Plan Worksheet
4.7	Mission Push-Up Possible	72	Intensity and progression	•		Mission Push-Up Possible Card
						Mission Push-Up Possible Chart
						Individual Push-Up Progress Sheet
4.8	Resistance Band Repetitions	75	Intensity and progression		•	Resistance Band Exercise Cards
						Resistance Band Log
4.9	Muscle Up	78	Specificity		•	Muscle Groups Diagram
						Muscle Up Classification Chart
4.10	R U on Overload?	81	Overload principle		•	Weight-Training Chart

4.1 Imposter—or Not?

MIDDLE SCHOOL

Muscular strength is the ability of a muscle or muscle group to exert a maximal force against a resistance through the full range of motion for a short period of time (it is important to emphasize "through the full range of motion" because any movement less than full range is counterproductive—strength or endurance gains occur only in the range of motion exercised). **Muscular endurance** is the ability of a muscle or muscle group to exert a submaximal force repeatedly over a period of time. Fewer repetitions of more-intense exercises are more likely to develop muscular strength, whereas more repetitions of less-intense exercises are more likely to develop muscular endurance.

PURPOSE

- Students will learn or review the definitions of muscular strength and muscular endurance.
- Students will practice identifying activities that develop muscular strength and endurance.
- Students will participate in a variety of muscular strength and endurance activities as well as other components of health-related fitness.

RELATIONSHIP TO NATIONAL STANDARDS

Physical Education Standard 4: Achieves and maintains a health-enhancing level of physical fitness.

Health Education Standard 1: Students will comprehend concepts related to health promotion and disease prevention.

EQUIPMENT

- Equipment as needed for stations
- Pencil, one per student
- Music and player

Reproducibles

- Imposter—or Not? Station Task Cards
- Imposter—or Not? Worksheet, one per student

Station 1

2 lower-body stretches

Activity 4.1   Imposter—Or Not? Station Task Cards
From Physical Best activity guide: Middle and high school levels, 2nd edition, by NASPE, 2005, Champaign, IL, Human Kinetics

Station 2

2 light resistance band exercises, 12 to 15 reps each

Activity 4.1   Imposter—Or Not? Station Task Cards
From Physical Best activity guide: Middle and high school levels, 2nd edition, by NASPE, 2005, Champaign, IL, Human Kinetics

Name: _____   Class: _____   Date: _____

Activity 4.1
Imposter—or Not? Worksheet

Some of the stations in today's activity build primarily muscular strength or muscular endurance, and some are focused on aerobic fitness or flexibility (the "imposters"). Write in the component of fitness emphasized most at each station on the "primary" line on the chart. If another component of fitness is emphasized to a lesser extent at that station, write it on the "secondary" line.
The choices for component of fitness are:
- Muscular strength
- Muscular endurance
- Aerobic fitness
- Flexibility

		Component of fitness	Imposter or not?
Station 1	Primary		
	Secondary		
Station 2	Primary		
	Secondary		
Station 3	Primary		
	Secondary		
Station 4	Primary		
	Secondary		
Station 5	Primary		
	Secondary		
Station 6	Primary		
	Secondary		
Station 7	Primary		
	Secondary		
Station 8	Primary		
	Secondary		

Activity 4.1   Imposter—or Not? Worksheet
From Physical Best activity guide: Middle and high school levels, 2nd edition, by NASPE, 2005, Champaign, IL, Human Kinetics

PROCEDURE

1. Create several stations that incorporate exercises for the different health-related fitness components: muscular strength, muscular endurance, aerobic fitness, and flexibility. (See the sidebar on page 58 for examples; make substitutions as your curriculum and supplies dictate.) Be sure you have at least one station each of the health-related fitness components. Two each of muscular strength and muscular endurance is more desirable. You can refer to other activities in this book for specific examples of exercises. One minute per station is a good guideline for timing the stations.

2. Discuss the definitions of muscular strength and muscular endurance with students. Brainstorm examples of physical activities that help enhance each and some that help enhance both.

3. Explain that today students will visit several stations and must identify the component of health-related fitness most emphasized at each station on their Imposter—or Not? Worksheets. If a secondary component is also developed through that activity, students will be asked to identify it as well. Students should further identify whether the exercise was an imposter activity or not. (Because this is a muscular strength and endurance activity, stations that focus on aerobic fitness and flexibility are imposters.)

4. Explain stations and reinforce safety rules as needed.

5. Divide students into small groups and assign one small group per station. Lead the entire class in a proper total-body warm-up before they begin the station work.

6. Send groups through each station, stopping music briefly to signal station changes. If the station has more than one activity, have students either choose one, or switch halfway through the station time.

7. Have groups repeat, or begin to repeat, stations if time allows.

8. Gather students into a large group for review and assessment.

© Human Kinetics

Imposter—Or not? Station Ideas

Station 1
Two lower body stretches (e.g., butterfly)

Station 2
Two light resistance band exercises, 12 to 15 reps each (e.g., biceps curls)

Station 3
Two light to medium intensity body-weight exercises (e.g., 12 to 15 curl-ups)

Station 4
Stepping, running in place, stationary cycling, or a similar activity

Station 5
Two upper body stretches (e.g., triceps stretch)

Station 6
Two medium resistance band exercises performed slowly for 6 to 8 reps (e.g., seated row)

TEACHING HINTS

- Create or discuss a station for which the whole class identifies a primary and a secondary health-related fitness component emphasized before having groups complete the stations on the worksheet (e.g., a jogging station primarily focuses on aerobic fitness but also helps develop muscular endurance of the legs).

- Remind students never to sacrifice proper form for speed because this can lead to injury.

- To use class time efficiently, place a supply of pencils and worksheets at each station for students to collect at the first station they complete.

SAMPLE INCLUSION TIPS

- If mobility or control is an issue for some students, allow them to substitute small hand weights in place of the resistance bands.

- For students with a cognitive or learning disability, have a peer leader for each station assist by providing physical or verbal cues and demonstration.

ASSESSMENT

- Verbally discuss the correct answers to the Imposter—or Not? Worksheet.

- Require individuals or partners to create a new station that develops muscular strength and/or endurance, and write a few sentences about how it does so. On another day, after a proper warm-up, have peers visit and perform other students' stations to evaluate how accurately the assignment was completed.

4.2 Go for the Team Gold

MIDDLE SCHOOL

Health benefits—Muscular strength and endurance activities are important in the musculoskeletal function of the body. When done properly, they improve body composition, bone density, and posture; prevent injuries; and help a person perform tasks of daily living and work.

PURPOSE

- Students will describe the benefits of muscular strength and endurance.
- Students will correctly perform the strength and endurance exercises.

RELATIONSHIP TO NATIONAL STANDARDS

Physical Education Standard 4: Achieves and maintains a health-enhancing level of physical fitness.

Physical Education Standard 5: Exhibits responsible personal and social behavior that respects self and others in physical activity settings.

Health Education Standard 1: Students will comprehend concepts related to health promotion and disease prevention.

EQUIPMENT

Proper equipment for performing the activities on the task cards, such as mats, curl-up strips, and so on

PROCEDURE

1. Review the role of strength training in not only providing strong muscles, but also assisting in correct posture, reducing low back pain, promoting a healthy body composition, and other benefits listed in the chapter introduction.

Reproducibles

- Go for the Team Gold Task Cards, at least one for every three students (In addition to the cards supplied on the CD-ROM, you can create your own task cards of other muscular strength activities with exercises listed. Corbin and Lindsey, *Fitness for Life,* 2005, is a good source.)
- Go for the Team Gold Handout (optional; see "Teaching Hints"), one per student

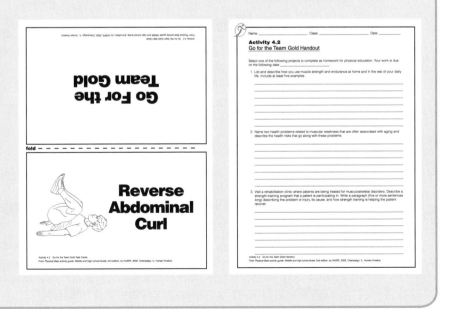

© Human Kinetics

2. Divide the class into small groups of three students each. Give each group one strength task from the Go for the Team Gold Task Cards and two to three minutes to discuss their exercise. Each group will describe how to perform the exercise, explain the health benefits of the exercise, and lead the group in a 30-second set of the exercise. Assign each member a responsibility or role such as the following:

- Strength trainer describes the exercise to the class.

- Medical expert explains the exercise benefits.

- Olympic athlete uses correct form and performs the exercise during the discussion.

3. Have each group in turn lead the entire class in a 30-second set of the exercises, allowing students to complete a 1-1 or 1-2 tempo cycle during the 30 seconds for 10 to 15 repetitions. (The focus on tempo is just as important for muscular strength and endurance development as performance technique. The 1-1 tempo cycle is 1-second concentric/eccentric movement. The 1-2 tempo cycle is 1-second concentric/2-second eccentric movement.)

TEACHING HINTS

■ Review the safety tips for strength training exercises including proper form and exhaling upon exertion.

■ The second time you teach this lesson, complete a continuous exercise routine, with students taking turns leading the exercise they led during the previous meeting.

■ Use the Go for the Team Gold Handout to extend this lesson into the community while reinforcing the concepts and literacy development.

■ Familiarize students with the task card activities through a previous lesson; circulate the room to assist as needed during the groups' two to three minute planning time.

SAMPLE INCLUSION TIPS

■ Develop task cards specific to students with physical disabilities. The cards should have muscular strength tasks that students with physical disabilities can do (e.g., biceps curls for a student who is in a wheelchair but has use of his or her arms).

■ Include pictures on task cards so that students with intellectual disabilities can easily interpret how to correctly perform the exercise.

ASSESSMENT

■ Have students explain how the benefits obtained from strength training extend beyond muscle development.

■ Have each student identify at least one health-related benefit from engaging in regular strength training activity.

■ Have each student gather three pictures from newspapers, magazines, or the Internet associated with the benefits of strength training as it assists health-related fitness (e.g., a teenager throwing a ball far, a construction worker lifting a cement block, an older person looking healthy and happy).

4.3 | Safely Finding the 8- to 12-Rep Range

HIGH SCHOOL

Intensity describes how hard a person exercises during a physical activity session. The appropriate intensity for an activity session depends on the age and fitness goals of the participant. Heart rate has traditionally been used as a measure of training intensity to develop aerobic fitness. When developing muscular strength and endurance, intensity is increased or decreased by adjusting the amount of resistance (weight) or number of repetitions.

PURPOSE

Students will learn how to safely determine an 8- to 12-rep range for each of at least two weight-training exercises (one upper body exercise and one lower body exercise).

RELATIONSHIP TO NATIONAL STANDARDS

Physical Education Standard 4: Achieves and maintains a health-enhancing level of physical fitness.

Physical Education Standard 5: Exhibits responsible personal and social behavior that respects self and others in physical activity settings.

Health Education Standard 1: Students will comprehend concepts related to health promotion and disease prevention.

EQUIPMENT

Variety of free weights and/or machine weights

PROCEDURE

1. Gather students and briefly introduce the rationale for the lesson—why we find the 8- to 12-rep set: It's an ideal range of repetitions for a muscular strength and endurance program. It provides an intensity that will allow for benefits to both muscular strength and muscular endurance while minimizing risk of injury.

2. Demonstrate or have a student (whose abilities you're sure of) demonstrate as follows:
   - Simulate that you're on the 7th rep and you're having trouble. Ask, "What should I do?" (Rest a minute, go to a lighter weight.)
   - Simulate that you're on the 13th rep and things are very easy. Ask, "What should I do?" (Go to a heavier weight.)

3. Remind students of the need for proper form and other safety rules. Make it clear

Reproducible

■ Weight-Training Chart

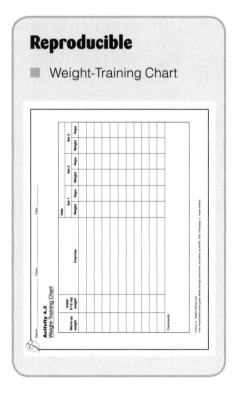

that a rep with proper form is the only type of rep that counts toward the 8- to 12-rep range. If you cannot maintain proper form, you are lifting too heavy a weight.

4. Explain today's procedure:

   • In groups of two to three at each station, warm up with very light weights for 30 seconds, only enough to get the motion for 8 to 12 reps (e.g., empty bar with a free weight or only one, two, or three pegs down [plates] on a weight machine). Use this warm-up weight to help you guess where you might reach fatigue in the 8- to 12-rep range.

   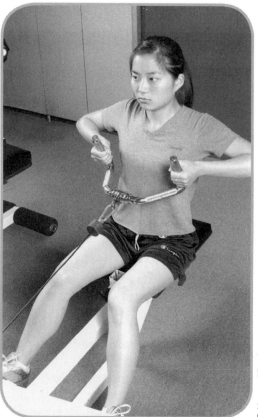

   • If you cannot lift at least 8 reps with proper form, rest one minute and try again at a lower weight. If you can lift more than 12, rest one minute, then try a heavier weight. Your partner can go while you rest, and you can spot each other. Help each other use proper form. There is a limit of 3 sets per exercise to find your 8- to 12-rep range. If you do not, adjust your weight 5 to 10 pounds up or down and write it down on your Weight-Training Chart for the next time.

5. Have students perform a general body warm-up for three to five minutes. Then release students to the weight stations or machines to do their weight-specific warm-up and range finding.

6. End class with an appropriate cool-down such as stretches specific to the exercises they've been performing.

TEACHING HINTS

■ Although it is considered ideal to find the weight at which a person can perform exactly 10 reps of an exercise (Baechle and Earle 2000), the 8- to 12-rep range is used in this lesson to increase safety through the following means:

   • Providing flexibility for students of varying abilities

   • Reducing the chance of fatigue by reducing the total number of sets a person must lift to find the range

   • Making it easier to judge a safe weight at which to start, limiting the likelihood that a person will lift a weight that is too heavy to be safe for him or her

■ Emphasize safety at all times:

   • Use only exercises for which students have previously learned proper form. Then closely monitor—and have peers monitor—proper form during the lesson.

   • Strongly discourage competition for the highest 8- to 12-rep ranges. Explain that the purpose of this lesson is to be able to use safe *lower* or *higher* weights in subsequent lessons to develop individual muscular endurance and strength (respectively), not to determine athletic prowess.

- Once students are familiar with their 8- to 12-rep ranges and are achieving adequate fitness levels, you may opt to explain and supervise students in gaining more strength at 6 to 10 reps or more endurance at 10 to 15 reps, depending on their needs and interests. Remember that the 8- to 12-rep range strikes a balance between both strength and endurance.
- Remember that students should *never* be asked or allowed to find 1RM (one-repetition maximum) during class time. Use common sense and *always* err on the side of safety when adapting this lesson to your students' abilities.

SAMPLE INCLUSION TIP

Strength training machines, seats, and benches serve as natural supports and boundaries for students with visual and physical impairments. As appropriate, allow peer to provide physical assistance to position student on bench press, leg press, wide grip pulldown or rows, shoulder press machines, and so on, prior to beginning any lifting.

ASSESSMENT

- Check students' use of the charts against the weights and reps they recorded on the Weight-Training Charts.
- Once you are sure each student has successfully determined the 8- to 12-rep range for each of the two exercises through this lesson, have students apply the knowledge by repeating the activity with another exercise or two.
- Determine students' ease of connecting the information in this lesson to finding safe warm-up weights in the activity titled Warm Up With Weights (pages 67-68); this may help you determine each student's understanding of this current lesson.

4.4 Rev-Up Roulette

MIDDLE SCHOOL

A **warm-up** increases the temperature of the body and the elasticity of the muscles. A warm-up improves the muscles' ability to perform work and reduces the risk of injury. A **cool-down** is the reverse process of the warm-up. A proper cool-down may reduce muscle soreness, help bring the body temperatures back to normal ranges, and allow muscles to flush wastes generated by exercise.

PURPOSE

- Students will understand that a general warm-up is essential for safe muscular strength and endurance training and need not include muscular strength and endurance activities.
- Students will see that warming up can be fun and cooling down can be both physically and emotionally relaxing.

RELATIONSHIP TO NATIONAL STANDARDS

Physical Education Standard 4: Achieves and maintains a health-enhancing level of physical fitness.

Health Education Standard 1: Students will comprehend concepts related to health promotion and disease prevention.

EQUIPMENT

- 2 game spinners (purchase at teacher supply store, take from a board game, or make your own. Attach to cardboard-mounted spinner found in the reproducibles on the CD-ROM.)
- Main muscular strength and endurance activity equipment (as desired)

Reproducible

- Rev-Up Roulette Warm-Up Spinner (attach to sturdy cardboard)
- Rev-Up Roulette Cool-Down Spinner (attach to sturdy cardboard)

Note: The spinners are left blank so that you can choose warm-up and cool-down activities personalized to your classes. Use your own ideas, and/or appropriate exercises from other warm-up/cool-down activities in this book.

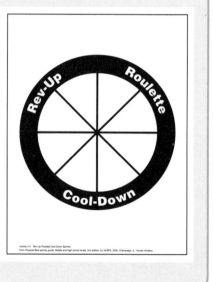

- Tape to attach spinners to activity area wall (optional)
- Upbeat and calming music and player (all optional)

PROCEDURE

© Human Kinetics

1. To begin warming up, select a student to spin the Rev-Up Roulette Warm-Up Spinner Wheel. The same or a different student leads the randomly selected warm-up activity.

2. Have students take turns spinning and leading until the class has warmed up for five or more minutes. As students move, have them call out the benefits of warming up before any health-related physical fitness activity. Guide students to gradually increase the intensity of repeated activities (e.g., if jogging comes up early on, encourage very slow jogging, such as challenging students to jog in slow motion; later encourage more intense jogging).

3. Briefly explain that whole-body activity is a safe way to get ready for the more specific muscular strength and endurance activities you will have students perform next.

4. Conduct the main muscular strength and endurance workout activities of your choice.

5. Repeat the spinning and leading of cool-down activities by using the Rev-Up Roulette Cool-Down Spinner. Emphasize the way stretching can help a person cool down after more intense activities, and should also be done with a warmed-up body (see also chapter 5 for more flexibility activity ideas and safety guidelines).

TEACHING HINTS

- Be sure to include goofy (but safe) activities—middle schoolers love them! Students can help with ideas, too, so you may want to include "free choice" on one or more sections of the spinner.
- Double or divide in half the time suggested for each activity, according to current needs and class attention span. However, never perform a stretch for less than 10 seconds.
- To maintain interest when warming up, keep the spinning and activities moving along steadily. For cool-downs, however, do not allow students to race through at expense of safety. Instead, emphasize the relaxation benefits of stretching.
- Middle school students love to talk, and the compulsion to do so is normal for the age group. Warm-up and cool-down are great times to let them do this as much as possible. How will this work when you want students to call out the benefits? Simply pause music or blow a whistle to signal students to yell out a benefit. It doesn't matter if they do so all at the same time, saying something different. They'll hear their neighbors and review the basics.
- Activity adaptations include rolling dice and numbering the spinner sections, in place of having an actual spinner, and dividing class into small groups with one spinner per group.

■ To increase students' chances to spin and lead, give each of your teams or squads a spinner so that they can spin for themselves. You can even have groups warm up at or next to an assigned workout station so that they'll already be at a station to begin the main workout.

SAMPLE INCLUSION TIP

Allow injured students to be involved as spinners.

ASSESSMENT

■ Have students tell you the benefits of warming up before muscular strength and endurance activities.

■ Ask, "How is cooling down physically beneficial? Why and how do you think it is helpful for you mentally or emotionally?"

4.5 Warm Up With Weights

HIGH SCHOOL

A **warm-up** increases the temperature of the body and the elasticity of the muscles. A warm-up improves the muscles' ability to perform work and reduces the risk of injury. A **cool-down** is the reverse process of the warm-up. A proper cool-down may reduce muscle soreness, help bring the body temperature back to normal ranges, and allow muscles to flush wastes generated by exercise.

Note: Students will need to know their 8- to 12-rep weights per exercise in order to calculate the weight for each exercise at which they can safely perform a warm-up. The activity titled Safely Finding 8- to 12-Rep Range (pages 61-63) contains an activity with guidelines for doing so.

PURPOSE

- Students will understand the importance, benefits, and procedure of warming up before and cooling down after muscular strength and endurance activities, in this case weight training.
- Students will figure out an individualized level of resistance for warm-ups and cool-downs.

RELATIONSHIP TO NATIONAL STANDARDS

Physical Education Standard 4: Achieves and maintains a health-enhancing level of physical fitness.

Physical Education Standard 5: Exhibits responsible personal and social behavior that respects self and others in physical activity settings.

Health Education Standard 1: Students will comprehend concepts related to health promotion and disease prevention.

EQUIPMENT

- Variety of free weights or machine weights
- Pencils, one per student

PROCEDURE

1. Discuss or review with students the importance and benefits of a properly conducted warm-up, especially with the higher resistance of weight training.

2. Divide students into pairs or small groups. Instruct groups to monitor each others' form and performance while encouraging each other to get the most out of the activity.

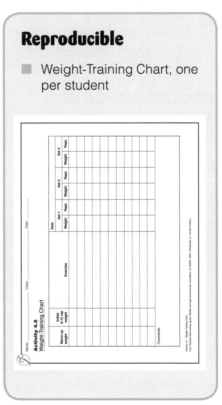

Reproducible

- Weight-Training Chart, one per student

3. Have students perform multiple-joint strength exercises for warming up. Appropriate exercises include bench presses; leg presses, lunges, or squats; wide-grip pulldowns or rows; and shoulder presses, as these each involve several muscle groups.

4. For each of the exercises selected, students should have previously determined the amount of weight they can properly handle for 8 to 12 repetitions (activity 4.3).

5. Direct them to then reduce that amount of weight by half for their "warm-up weight." For example, if a student can do 10 reps with 60 pounds, the student's warm-up weight would be 30 pounds.

6. Direct students to record their individual warm-up weights for each exercise on their Weight-Training Charts. Have them refer to these weights each time they warm up before a strength training workout.

7. For a cool-down, have students use the same amount of weight as was calculated for the warm-up. Also incorporate flexibility exercises that are specific to the muscle groups being used in each exercise.

TEACHING HINTS

- Be sure students warm up and cool down each time they work out, to develop the habit.

- Alternate and modify the exercises you choose for warm-ups and cool-downs based on your equipment and student needs.

- Caution students against lifting free weights without a spotter if they plan to strength train outside of class.

SAMPLE INCLUSION TIP

Have students trade charts with each other to check that they calculated their warm-up weights correctly, prior to performing the warm-up.

ASSESSMENT

- At the conclusion of the lesson, ask students to list the importance, benefits, and procedures of properly warming up and cooling down.

- Review students' weight charts for their warm-up information. Make sure they have calculated reasonably low weights to prevent injury.

- Have students choose a favorite physical activity and write a proper warm-up and cool-down routine for the activity, based on the principles learned.

- Include questions on the importance, benefits, and procedures of warming up and cooling down on a strength training unit test.

- Ask students how having a partner or small group might help them work on strength training outside of class time (e.g., motivation, encouragement, proper form). Ask this during a class discussion or when monitoring groups, or have students record their thoughts in a journal.

4.6 Muscles in Action

MIDDLE SCHOOL

The principle of **specificity** states that to bring about changes in a particular body system, muscle, or skill, a person must perform activities that target that particular body system, muscle, or skill.

PURPOSE

- Students will identify the location of the following muscles and muscle groups: trapezius, deltoid, pectorals, latissimus dorsi, obliques, gluteus maximus, rectus abdominis, quadriceps, hamstrings, gastrocnemius, triceps, and biceps, and select exercises for those muscles.
- Students will be able to name the muscle when shown its location on the body.

RELATIONSHIP TO NATIONAL STANDARDS

Physical Education Standard 4: Achieves and maintains a health-enhancing level of physical fitness.

Physical Education Standard 5: Exhibits responsible personal and social behavior that respects self and others in physical activity settings.

Health Education Standard 1: Students will comprehend concepts related to health promotion and disease prevention.

Health Education Standard 3: Students will demonstrate the ability to practice health-enhancing behaviors and reduce health risks.

EQUIPMENT

- Masking tape for each group
- Folders, which will each contain a Labeled Muscle Diagram; one folder for every three students

PROCEDURE

1. Before class, tape the Muscles in Action Exercise Posters on one wall of the activity area, evenly spacing them. Explain that today the students will be putting their muscles into action by creating a "Muscle Model" and a plan for exercising those muscles.

2. Divide students into groups of three. Give each group a set of laminated Muscle Cards. Direct each group to select one person to model the Muscle Cards, that is, to become the muscle model. The other two group members alternate taping the laminated cards to the correct muscle location on their muscle model.

3. When all 12 Muscle Cards have been placed on the model, one group member asks the teacher for the folder with the Labeled Muscle Diagram. The group uses the diagram to check the accuracy of the muscle cards they taped to their muscle model. Any incorrectly placed Muscle Cards must be corrected.

4. When a group feels confident that each member can identify the location of all 12 muscles, they return the Muscle Cards and diagram folder to the teacher, who gives each student a Muscles in Action Plan Worksheet.

Reproducibles

- Muscles in Action Exercise Posters
- Muscle Cards, one set for every three students
- Labeled Muscle Diagram, one per folder (every three students)
- Muscles in Action Plan Worksheet, one per student

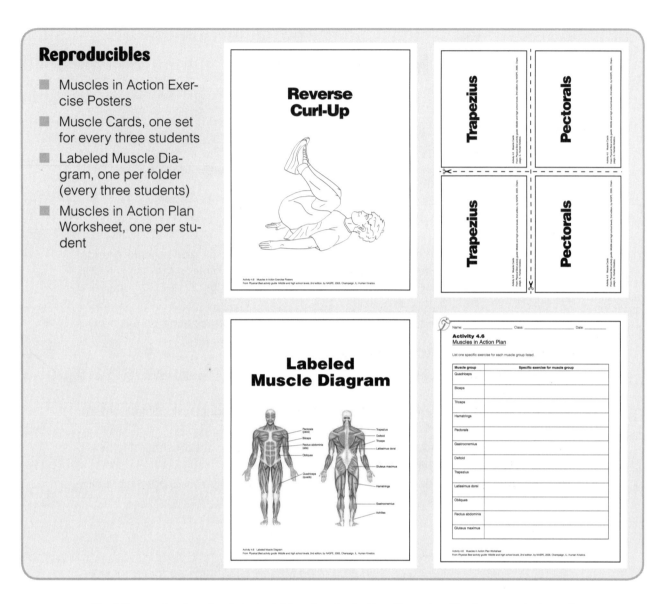

5. After reviewing the labeled Muscles in Action Exercise Posters posted on the wall, each student designs a personal Muscles in Action Plan by selecting one exercise for each muscle or muscle group listed on the plan.

6. When all members of the group have completed their Muscles in Action Plan, students in the group alternate leading their group in the selected exercises.

7. Students need to keep their plans in their fitness portfolios.

8. In a large group discuss (1) which muscle locations and names are most difficult to remember; (2) which exercises are favorites; and (3) how to best use the Muscle in Action Plans.

TEACHING HINTS

- If students are not already familiar with the muscle groups and exercises, select a few to focus on at each class—and complete the activity over two or three class periods.
- Laminate the exercise pictures and muscle diagrams.
- Encourage students to be respectful when placing the Muscle Cards on the models.

- If students' touching each other creates a management problem, form same-sex groups, and ask models to attach cards themselves, based on peer instructions.

SAMPLE INCLUSION TIP

This activity introduces the identification of very specific anatomical/physiological body parts. It is extremely important for all students to begin to develop the initial concepts of personal body image. Students with cognitive/learning disabilities may have a peer buddy assist them in identifying a general locale to a specific muscle group—such as touching the body part and giving a generally acceptable muscle name or anatomical site for the more specific name (i.e., pectorals as pecs or chest muscles; deltoids as shoulder muscles; obliques as abdominals).

ASSESSMENT

- Point to a specific exercise picture and ask students to identify the muscle group worked.
- Name a muscle group and ask students to demonstrate one exercise designed to affect that muscle group.

4.7 Mission Push-Up Possible

MIDDLE SCHOOL

Intensity describes how hard a person exercises during a physical activity session. The appropriate intensity for an activity session depends on the age and fitness goals of the participant. When developing muscular strength and endurance, intensity is increased or decreased by adjusting the amount of resistance (weight) and/or number of repetitions. **Progression** refers to how an individual increases the overload, thereby placing greater-than-normal demands on the musculature of the body. The level of exercise should be gradually increased and may be manipulated by increasing the frequency, intensity, time, or a combination of all three components. In muscular strength and endurance training, progression involves a systematic approach to increasing the resistance and intensity of the activity.

PURPOSE

- Students will identify and perform push-ups that are appropriate for their individual fitness level.
- Students will explain how the principles of intensity and progression apply to this activity.

RELATIONSHIP TO NATIONAL STANDARDS

Physical Education Standard 3: Participates regularly in physical activity.

Physical Education Standard 4: Achieves and maintains a health-enhancing level of physical fitness.

Physical Education Standard 5: Exhibits responsible personal and social behavior that respects self and others in physical activity settings.

Physical Education Standard 6: Values physical activity for health, enjoyment, challenge, self-expression and/or social interaction.

Health Education Standard 1: Students will comprehend concepts related to health promotion and disease prevention.

Health Education Standard 3: Student will demonstrate the ability to practice health-enhancing behaviors and reduce health risks.

EQUIPMENT

- Large envelopes with "Mission Push-Up Possible" written on the outside in large letters, one envelope for every three to four students
- 2 colored markers in each envelope
- Chairs, one for every three to four students
- Benches, one for every three to four students
- Mats, one for every three to four students
- Chart paper, one sheet for every three to four students
- Wall tape (to secure chart paper to wall)
- Optional: *Mission Impossible* music and player

Reproducibles

- Mission Push-Up Possible Card, one per envelope
- Mission Push-Up Possible Chart, one per envelope
- Individual Push-Up Progress Sheet, one per student

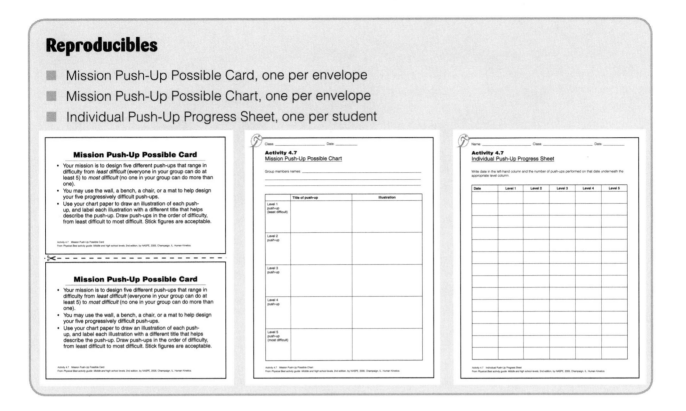

PROCEDURE

1. Review the concepts of intensity and progression, providing several examples.

2. Divide students into groups of three to four. Give each group a Mission Push-Up Possible envelope. Review the Mission Push-Up Possible Card that is in each group's envelope. Each group will design five different push-ups that range in difficulty from least difficult to most difficult. Encourage all students to experiment with different types of push-ups. Emphasize that students are determining their baseline for push-ups, that this is not a competition, and that everyone is capable of progressing to higher-level push-ups if they carefully apply the fitness principles of intensity and progression.

3. Post a large version of the Mission Push-Up Possible Chart for all to see.

4. Allow groups time to create their Push-Up Progression Charts, illustrating the five push-ups they have designed (see the instructions on the Mission Push-Up Possible Cards).

5. Ask students to post their group's chart of push-up illustrations on the wall, leaving about six feet between each chart. If wall space is not available, secure charts by other means—such as to the back of a chair, or in slotted cones.

6. After a group's chart is posted, ask each student in the group to select the push-up level that best matches his or her fitness level. Each student attempts to perform at least 10 repetitions of the selected push-up, while maintaining proper form.

7. When a student can perform more than 10 push-ups at a given level, the student may move to the next level. If a student cannot perform 10 push-ups at a given level, the student should stay at that level until they can perform 10 push-ups.

© Human Kinetics

8. Give each student an Individual Push-Up Possible Progress Sheet to document progress over a period of several weeks. Have students keep their sheets in a fitness portfolio or other organizer for future use.

9. Ask each group to share their most creative push-ups with the class. Discuss the principles of progression and intensity as they relate to this activity.

TEACHING HINTS

■ Provide a list of push-ups such as: High-Five Push-Up; Wall Push-Up; Clap in Between; Hands Close Together; Hands Far Apart; Crossed-Leg Push-Up; Knee Push-Up; Incline Push-Up.

■ Ask students to review all groups' Mission Possible Push-Up Charts and collectively select seven or eight progressively difficult push-ups that can become the Class Push-Up Chart.

SAMPLE INCLUSION TIPS

There are a variety of ways a student with a disability can perform push-ups.

■ For students using wheelchairs, allow the student to remain in the chair and perform wheelchair push-ups (release chair seatbelt, allow student to position himself as needed, student places hands on arm rests, pushes self up and lowers self down with control; repeat as many as possible).

■ Students who cannot support their weight with their arms might do variations of biceps curls, arm circles, or triceps extensions.

■ For students with limited upper body strength, allow student to perform bent leg push-ups or standing push-ups in an inclined position against the wall.

ASSESSMENT

■ Review the students' Individual Push-Up Progress Sheets:
  • Is each student recording progress on the sheet?
  • Is each student making progress?

■ Have students pair with a class member and share how the push-up activity relates to the principles of intensity and progression. Randomly call on pairs to share their thoughts with the entire class.

4.8 Resistance Band Repetitions

HIGH SCHOOL

Intensity describes how hard a person exercises during a physical activity session. The appropriate intensity for an activity session depends on the age and fitness goals of the participant. When developing muscular strength and endurance, intensity is increased or decreased by adjusting the amount of resistance (weight) and/or the number of repetitions. **Progression** refers to how an individual increases the overload, thereby placing greater-than-normal demands on the musculature of the body. The level of exercise should be gradually increased and may be manipulated by increasing the frequency, intensity, time, or a combination of all three components. In muscular strength and endurance training, progression involves a systematic approach to increasing the resistance and intensity of the activity. Using heavier resistance and fewer repetitions improves strength. Using lighter resistance with more repetitions improves endurance.

PURPOSE

- Students will understand the concepts of intensity and progression as applied to muscular strength and endurance.
- Students will practice personal responsibility and leadership through teaching their peers.

RELATIONSHIP TO NATIONAL STANDARDS

Physical Education Standard 3: Participates regularly in physical activity.

Physical Education Standard 4: Achieves and maintains a health-enhancing level of physical fitness.

Physical Education Standard 5: Exhibits responsible personal and social behavior that respects self and others in physical activity settings.

Health Education Standard 3: Students will demonstrate the ability to practice health-enhancing behaviors and reduce health risks.

Health Education Standard 5: Students will demonstrate the ability to use interpersonal communication skills to enhance health.

EQUIPMENT

- Mats, one per student
- Resistance bands or resistance tubing of various colors (strength of resistance), at least one per student
- Pencils, one per student

PROCEDURE

1. Discuss *resistance* and *repetition* as they relate to *intensity* and *progression* in muscle strength and endurance training.
2. Place mats in a large circle, laying out resistance bands of varying resistance.
3. Divide students into pairs or small groups, and give each group a Resistance Band Exercise Card. Direct groups to learn and practice the exercise on their card.

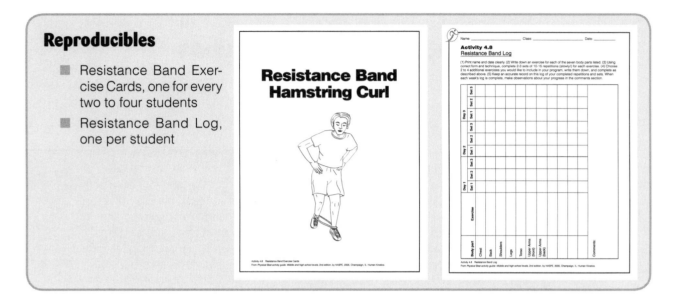

Reproducibles

- Resistance Band Exercise Cards, one for every two to four students
- Resistance Band Log, one per student

Resistance Band Hamstring Curl

Activity 4.8   Resistance Band Exercise Cards
From *Physical Best activity guide: Middle and high school levels, 2nd edition,* by NASPE, 2005, Champaign, IL: Human Kinetics.

Name: _____ Class: _____ Date: _____

Activity 4.8
Resistance Band Log

(1) Print name and date clearly. (2) Write down an exercise for each of the seven body parts listed. (3) Using correct form and technique, complete 2-3 sets of 10-15 repetitions (slowly) for each exercise. (4) Choose 2 to 4 additional exercises you would like to include in your program, write them down, and complete as described above. (5) Keep an accurate record on this log of your completed repetitions and sets. When each week's log is complete, make observations about your progress in the comments section.

Activity 4.8   Resistance Band Log
From *Physical Best activity guide: Middle and high school levels, 2nd edition,* by NASPE, 2005, Champaign, IL: Human Kinetics.

4. Once groups have learned their exercise, ask them to figure out (1) how they could increase and decrease the intensity of their exercise and (2) how they could apply the concept of progression over a period of time with this exercise.

5. When groups are ready, have them lead the class through one set of 10 to 15 repetitions. The group should name the muscles worked, explain how intensity could be increased and decreased, and explain how they could apply the concept of progression over a period of time with the exercise.

6. Give each student a Resistance Band Log, and have students keep track of their resistance band exercises over time.

TEACHING HINTS

- If preferred, provide each group with a packet of all the exercises to be learned, allowing each group to work and learn independently. This would eliminate the peer-coaching element but may work better in certain situations. Alternatively, you could teach each exercise to the entire group first. Then in subsequent lessons, have the students work in pairs or independently.

- Consult physical education catalogs and resistance band books to add new exercises to this activity.

SAMPLE INCLUSION TIPS

- For students with low fitness levels, in addition to developing muscular strength and endurance, resistance bands can also increase range of motion. For students unable to grasp resistance bands, use hand-over-hand assistance for movements.

■ Position students with visual or auditory impairments in such a way as to see and hear the other groups' demonstrations.

ASSESSMENT

■ Ask students to describe how resistance and repetition can be used to create intensity and progression in muscle development.

■ Ask students, "How would you adjust intensity and progression to achieve increased muscular strength?" "How would you adjust intensity and progression to achieve muscular endurance?"

■ Tie in specificity by asking volunteers to demonstrate an exercise they learned today (from another group) and the muscle group it works.

■ Use the Resistance Band Log over a period of classes, and note any improvements in resistance and repetitions.

4.9 Muscle Up

HIGH SCHOOL

The principle of **specificity** states that to bring about changes in a particular body system, muscle, or skill, a person must perform activities that target that particular body system, muscle, or skill.

PURPOSE

- Students will identify muscles used to improve specific skills.
- Students will describe the principle of specificity.

RELATIONSHIP TO NATIONAL STANDARDS

Physical Education Standard 4: Achieves and maintains a health-enhancing level of physical fitness.

Physical Education Standard 5: Exhibits responsible personal and social behavior that respects self and others in physical activity settings.

Health Education Standard 1: Students will comprehend concepts related to health promotion and disease prevention.

EQUIPMENT

- Pencils, one per student
- The following items are specific to the sample stations offered in the procedures; substitute as needed.
  - Medicine ball
  - Hand weights
  - Resistance bands or resistance tubing
  - Floor tape

Reproducibles

- Muscle Groups Diagram, one per station, if possible
- Muscle Up Classification Chart, one per student

Muscle Groups Diagram

Activity 4.9 Muscle Groups Diagram
From Physical Best activity guide: Middle and high school levels, 2nd edition, by NASPE, 2005, Champaign, IL: Human Kinetics.

Name _____ Class _____ Date _____

Activity 4.9
Muscle Up Classification Chart

Complete the blanks at each station.

Station	Primary muscles used	Sport skill targeted at station
1		
2		
3		
4		
5		
6		
7		
8		
9		
10		

Activity 4.9 Muscle Up Classification Chart
From Physical Best activity guide: Middle and high school levels, 2nd edition, by NASPE, 2005, Champaign, IL: Human Kinetics.

- Cones
- Balance boards
- Volleyballs or basketballs

PROCEDURE

1. Before class, set up 10 stations around the perimeter of the activity area. As an example, refer to the sidebar titled "Activity Station Suggestions for Basketbal" on page 80. Leave the center area open for aerobic activity. Briefly review the major muscle groups using the muscle groups diagram and the principle of specificity.

2. Distribute a Muscle Up Classification Chart and a pencil to each student. Explain that the charts will be completed as the student progresses through the stations.

3. Divide students into 10 small groups and assign each group to a different station. Explain that students will rotate clockwise to the next station every two minutes.

4. After groups have completed two or three stations, signal them to move to the aerobic area and perform a selected aerobic activity for two to three minutes.

5. Have students return to the stations and continue progressing through them, rotating to an aerobic activity after every two or three stations are completed.

6. Ask students to share and discuss their Muscle Up Classification Charts within their groups.

TEACHING HINTS

- You can use this activity as a springboard for any sport. The key is for the stations to emphasize the primary muscles used in that sport.

- Tape music in two-minute segments to accommodate the station changes. Playing it will also increase motivation.

© Human Kinetics

SAMPLE INCLUSION TIPS

- Decrease time or intensity of certain activities. For example: use lighter weights or no weights or substitute various sizes of beanbags as hand weights.

- Activity stations designed to self-challenge and self-test students with behavioral and emotional disorders are considered developmentally appropriate activities for this population.

ASSESSMENT

- Monitor the small group discussions of the Muscle Up Classification Charts.

- In a large group, discuss students' work on the classification chart and respond to questions or errors.

- Ask students to write a definition of specificity and an example of specificity on a separate sheet of paper or in their fitness portfolios.

Activity Station Suggestions for Basketball

The following stations can be used to develop muscular strength and endurance and motor skills specific to basketball.

Medicine Ball Pass
Students chest-pass medicine ball to each other.

Lateral Slides and Vertical Jumps
Set up four to five obstacles for students to slide around. After they have completed slides, have students move to the closest wall where you have placed six 4-inch pieces of tape on the wall at varying heights. Students progress through the tape area, jumping six times, each time attempting to better the height of their previous jump.

Wrist Curls
Using hand weights or resistance bands, students perform sets of 10 wrist curls and 10 reverse wrist curls.

Wall Sit
Students maintain a wall-sit position for as long as possible.

Rebound
Students chest-pass a ball against the wall and continually rebound their tosses.

Squat Jumps
Students perform as many squat jumps as possible for two minutes.

Agility Drill
Use gym tape to outline a ladder on the floor. Ask students to jump with both feet "up and down" the ladder without stepping on the tape. Have them perform both laterally and straight forward and backward.

Dot Drill
Using the dot drill pattern, ask students to perform it as quickly and accurately as possible. (Dot drills are used for agility and leg strength/muscle endurance. The student would stand on two dots that are spread about 2 feet apart, then jump back with both feet together, then jump back again with legs spread. Then they would jump forward with feet together again, then forward with legs apart again. They would perform this activity going forward and backward as quickly and accurately as possible.)

Balance Drill
Use balance boards, or ask students to hold the following poses: stork stand with eyes open, then eyes closed; one leg up at 90 degrees with eyes open, then closed; rise up on toes and hold.

Deltoid Drill
Have students perform a series of lifts that strengthen the deltoids (e.g., shoulder presses, lateral raises, front raises, rear raises). They can use either hand weights or resistance bands.

4.10 R U on Overload?

HIGH SCHOOL

The **overload principle** states that a body system (cardiorespiratory, muscular, or skeletal) must perform at a level beyond normal in order to adapt and improve physiological function and fitness.

PURPOSE

- Students will use their knowledge of their 8- to 12-rep range estimates to carefully apply the principle of overload.
- Students will reinforce their understanding of 8- to 12-rep range and the principle of progression.

RELATIONSHIP TO NATIONAL STANDARDS

Physical Education Standard 3: Participates regularly in physical activity.

Physical Education Standard 4: Achieves and maintains a health-enhancing level of physical fitness.

Physical Education Standard 5: Exhibits responsible personal and social behavior that respects self and others in physical activity settings.

Health Education Standard 1: Students will comprehend concepts related to health promotion and disease prevention.

Health Education Standard 3: Student will demonstrate the ability to practice health-enhancing behaviors and reduce health risks.

EQUIPMENT

Various free weights and machine weights

PROCEDURE

Prior to the activity:
Students will need to know their 8- to 12-rep weights per exercise (see Activity 4.3) in order to calculate the weight for each exercise at which they can safely perform a warm-up (see Activity 4.5). In addition, follow these guidelines for safety:

1. Carefully assess each student's understanding of previous lessons, especially 4.3 (Safely Finding the 8- to 12-Rep Range) and 4.5 (Warm-Up With Weights).

2. Be willing and vigilant in enforcing weight-training safety rules.

3. Require students to get your approval of their R U on Overload? plans before implementing them. This will allow you time to

Reproducible

- Weight-Training Chart (one per student)

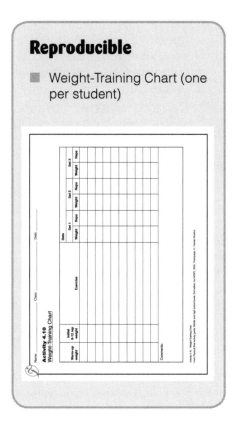

assess whether or not each student has created an appropriate, safe plan for applying the principle of overload.

During the activity:

1. Briefly remind students of the safety rules of weightlifting. Discuss or review the principle of overload.

2. Simulate or have a student (whose abilities you're familiar with and is warmed-up) demonstrate finding the 8- to 12-rep range. Ask, "What must I do to lower my rep range to 6 to 10?" (Lift a heavier weight.) Simulate lifting 6 to 10 reps in a heavier range, emphasizing that you should not increase the weight much. Ask, "If I can still reach eleven or more reps, what should I do?" (Rest one minute, and move to a heavier weight.) Again, emphasize the need to move to a heavier weight cautiously, in small increments. Ask, "If I can't lift six reps, what should I do?" (Rest one minute and move to a lighter weight.)

3. Now simulate what happens when students regularly work on muscular strength—they'll be able to lift more reps. Ask, "What do I do now?" (Increase the weight and find a new weight you can lift 6 to 10 reps of.) State, "This applies the principle of progression. When you lift a weight regularly, your muscles build strength, then you **progress** to a new weight in order to keep applying the principle of overload *and* the principle of progression."

4. Have students perform a warm-up, using their prerecorded warm-up weights.

5. Direct students to use their initial 8-12 rep weight recorded on their Weight-Training Charts to help them choose how to increase their weights slowly. Emphasize that students will only find their 6- to 10-rep range for one lower body and one upper body exercise today. In the future, they will find others, but gradually building up strength is vital to preventing injury. Tell students to record their 6- to 10-rep weights in the corresponding column, but to circle these numbers to indicate they are applying the overload principle.

6. Send students to stations or machines in groups of two or three. Continue with the weight-training session by having students complete the circuit using the 8- to 12-rep range.

7. Close the lesson with an appropriate cooldown, such as stretches specific to the exercises performed during the lesson.

TEACHING HINTS

© Human Kinetics

- When first using this lesson, have students find their overload (6- to 10-rep) range for only one exercise for the upper body and one for the lower body. Gradually have students apply the principle of overload to other exercises over time, alternating leg and arm muscle groups.

- Continually (and have peers) monitor safety procedures, including proper form, competition ban, and storage of equipment between uses.

- Monitor students' application of the principle of overload over an extended period to ensure progression is gradual and muscular soreness and other injuries are minimized.

■ Often instructors think that student-athletes do not need to do this activity or do not think that student-athletes are too challenged by it. However, except when resting in preparation for a special meet or game, the student-athlete can learn just as much from this lesson as any other student.

■ For students who prefer to focus on muscular endurance, after teaching the initial lesson, to teach the overload concept for muscular strength, allow them to focus more on increasing repetitions.

SAMPLE INCLUSION TIP

Ensure that students with injuries or physical disabilities get to perform exercises by using muscle groups for which they have the most confidence and control.

ASSESSMENT

■ Require students to submit a plan detailing how they will apply the principle of overload to another weight-training exercise. Be sure to review and approve the proposals.

■ Ask students to predict the number of reps they will be able to do if they work out regularly, if they currently do those same exercises at 6 to 10 reps. More or fewer? (More, because their strength builds up.)

5

Flexibility

Chapter Contents

Flexibility is the ability to move a joint through its complete range of motion (ACSM 2000). The goal is to develop and maintain normal joint range of motion. Keep in mind that having too much mobility predisposes people to injury and therefore can be as potentially detrimental as having too little.

Flexibility can bring about many benefits:

- Decreased muscle tension and increased relaxation (I can sleep better)
- Greater ease of movement (I can move easier)
- Improved coordination (I can perform better in sport or dance)
- Increased range of motion (I can bend, stretch, and twist into many positions)
- Reduced risk of injury (I can move safely)
- Better body awareness and postural alignment (I have good posture)
- Improved circulation and air exchange (I can breathe easier)
- Smoother and easier contractions (My muscles work better)
- Decreased muscle soreness (I am less sore after leisure activities)
- Possible prevention of low back pain and other spinal problems (I can sit through my day at school without my back feeling sore)
- Improved personal appearance and self-image (I feel good about myself)
- Facilitates the development and maintenance of motor skills (I can participate in a variety of activities)

Defining Flexibility

There are two types of flexibility (*static* and *dynamic*) with four types of stretches (*static, active, PNF,* and *passive*) that foster the development of flexibility and improved range of motion.

- **Static flexibility** is defined as the range of motion at a joint or group of joints.
- **Dynamic (ballistic) flexibility** is the rate of increase in tension in a relaxed muscle as it is stretched (Knudson, Magnusson, and McHugh 2000).
- A **static stretch** is a slow, sustained stretch of the muscle, held for 10 to 30 seconds. The person stretches the muscle-tendon unit to the point of mild discomfort then backs off slightly (holding the stretch at a point just prior to discomfort).
- In an **active stretch**, the person stretching provides the force of the stretch (for example, in the sit-and-reach, the person leans forward and reaches as far as possible). (See figure 7.2a in *Physical Education for Lifelong Fitness: The Physical Best Teacher's Guide, Second Edition.*)
- In a **passive stretch**, a partner provides the force of the stretch (see figure 7.2b in *Physical Education for Lifelong Fitness: The Physical Best Teacher's Guide, Second Edition*).
- **Proprioceptive neuromuscular facilitation (PNF)** is a static stretch using combinations of the active and passive stretching techniques. Pubescent and postpubescent students as well as those who have developed a solid base of training and are undergoing formal athletic conditioning from a qualified coach can perform this type of stretch (Bompa 2000). Safety, proper instruction, and responsibility are key issues in performing the PNF stretch. Injury may result when students are not responsible or fail to listen to the cues of their partners, thereby forcing a stretch, or incorrectly perform a stretch.

Teaching Guidelines for Flexibility

As in all areas of health-related fitness, the principles of training (progression, overload, specificity, regularity, and individuality) must be applied. The FITT Guidelines (table 5.1) also play a key role in improving flexibility.

In applying the principles of training and the FITT Guidelines, be aware of the factors that affect flexibility (see *Physical Education for Lifelong Fitness: The Physical Best Teacher's Guide, Second Edition*) and therefore the improvement you may or may not observe.

Training Methods for Flexibility

Choose a variety of flexibility exercises and a variety of avenues to teach flexibility concepts to prevent boredom and the drudgery of performing the same old stretches day after day. This is also the time to explain the relationship between flexibility exercises performed in class with the back-saver sit-and-reach test and shoulder stretch test (*FITNESSGRAM*) performed during the fitness assessment portion of your program. When teaching flexibility concepts, stress safety and proper technique. Students should use slow, controlled movements when stretching, holding each stretch to the point of mild discomfort (and perhaps backing off slightly) for 10 to 30 seconds. Holding the stretch at the point of discomfort and backing off slightly ensure application of the overload principle.

Other safety precautions include the following:

- Avoid locking any joint (soft knees, soft joints)
- Do not overstretch a joint (pay attention to the tightness felt during the stretch)
- Never stretch the neck or spine too far
- Do not perform ballistic stretches (reserved for controlled, sport-specific training of secondary students and adults)
- A trained health care professional should check a student who has excessive mobility

Along with these safety precautions, be aware of questionable exercises or contraindicated exercises as presented in the *Physical Education for Lifelong Fitness: The Physical Best Teacher's Guide, Second Edition*.

TABLE 5.1 FITT Guidelines Applied to Flexibility

Frequency	Three times per week, preferably daily and after a warm-up to raise muscle temperature.
Intensity	Slow elongation of the muscle to the point of mild discomfort and back off slightly.
Time	Up to 4-5 stretches per muscle or muscle group. Hold each stretch 10-30 sec. Always warm-up properly prior to stretching.
Type	The preferred stretch for the classroom is slow static stretching for all muscles or muscle groups.

NOTE: Although 10-30 sec is recommended as the length of time to hold a stretch, an advanced student may hold a stretch up to 60 sec.

Modified from Knudson, D.V., P. Magnusson, and M. McHugh. (2000). Current issues in flexibility fitness. In C. Corbin and B. Pangrazi, eds., *The president's council on physical fitness and sports digest,* 3rd ser., no. 10, Washington, DC: Department of Health and Human Services.

Modified from American College of Sports Medicine (ACSM). 2001. *ACSM's Resource manual for guidelines for exercise testing and prescription.* 4th ed. Philadelphia: Lippincott, Williams, and Wilkins.

Factors That Affect Flexibility

- Failure to adhere to a regular program
- Muscle temperature
- Age and gender (Knudson, Magnusson, and McHugh 2000)
- Tissue interference (Heyward 2002)
- Muscle tension
- Poor coordination and strength during active movement
- Pain
- Lack of proper warm-up (Alter 1998; Knudson, Magnusson, and McHugh 2000)
- Certain diseases (Blanchard 1999)

Flexibility is an important component of health-related fitness, so resist the temptation to always relegate it to warm-ups and cool-downs. The activities that follow provide several opportunities to use flexibility as the focus of your lesson or to add variety to your warm-ups and cool-downs.

Motor Skill Development Through Flexibility Activities

Normal full range of motion (ROM) is essential to learning and perfecting motor skills, and a student with limited ROM will have greater difficulty mastering a motor skill that a classmate with normal mobility will learn easily. The specificity principle applies here. For example, if a student wants to be able to punt a football or perform a high kick in a soccer game, he or she must have good leg flexibility. Good flexibility, then, enhances motor skill development.

Motor skill development through fitness activity is the perfect area for you to consider the abilities and disabilities of all students. Some are high achievers, others are low achievers, and still others have physical or intellectual disabilities. Provide opportunities for all students to develop physical skills and be successful in your classroom. If a student has a severe disability, you may need to contact a person who specializes in adapted physical education for assistance in developing an individualized education plan.

When students see the connections between flexibility and the physical activities they are engaging in, they are more likely to continue working on enhancing flexibility as a lifestyle choice. In short, you create a deeper awareness of the need for flexibility.

Activities

Chapter 5 Activities Grid

Activity number	Activity title	Activity page	Concept	Middle school	High school	Reproducible (on CD-Rom)
5.1	Flexibility Fling	90	Definition	●		Flexibility Task and Benefit Cards
						Unsafe Stretching Risk Cards
5.2	All-Star Stretches	92	Health benefits	●	●	Flexibility Task and Benefit Cards
						Unsafe Stretching Risk Cards
						Guidelines for Safe Stretching Poster
5.3	Type Cast	95	Specificity	●	●	Flexibility Task and Benefit Cards
						Benefits of Good Flexibility Poster
5.4	Sport Spectacular	98	Specificity		●	Sport Stretch Pages
5.5	Introduction to Yoga	100	Frequency and time	●	●	Yoga Signs
						Yoga Pose Cards
						Yoga Log

5.1 Flexibility Fling

MIDDLE SCHOOL
Good **flexibility** is the ability to move a joint through a complete range of motion.

PURPOSE

- Students will learn or review the definition of flexibility while learning or reviewing 12 stretches for a variety of muscles and joints.
- Students will identify two unsafe stretching practices.

RELATIONSHIP TO NATIONAL STANDARDS

Physical Education Standard 4: Achieves and maintains a health-enhancing level of physical fitness.

Health Education Standard 1: Students will comprehend concepts related to health promotion and disease prevention.

EQUIPMENT

- 1 large cardboard box
- 1 Frisbee
- Mats (optional)

PROCEDURE

1. Set up the box at the front of the activity area. Place five of the Flexibility Task and Benefit Cards and the two Unsafe Stretching Risk Cards in the box. Keep the other five Flexibility Task and Benefit Cards in your possession.

2. After performing a warm-up activity, briefly review the definition of good flexibility and discuss safe stretching practices. Explain that today students will be learning (or reviewing) 10 stretches that, together, may enhance performance across

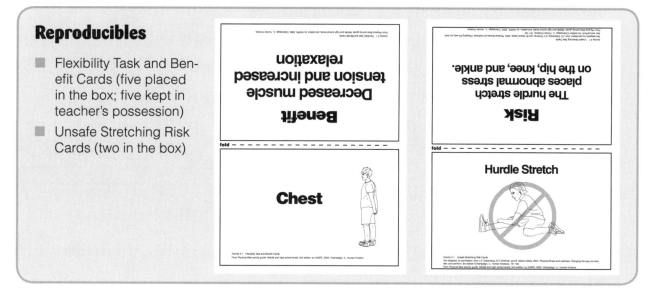

Reproducibles

- Flexibility Task and Benefit Cards (five placed in the box; five kept in teacher's possession)
- Unsafe Stretching Risk Cards (two in the box)

© Human Kinetics

a variety of sports and physical activities. However, there are also two additional stretches in the mix that show unsafe practices. Students will have to be alert to not perform these. Instead, they will call out, "Unsafe! Unsafe!"

3. Choose a volunteer to throw the Frisbee from a distance into the box. If the Frisbee lands in the box, the student selects one card. Have the student lead the stretch (or lead the class in calling out, "Unsafe!"). If the Frisbee lands outside the box, the stretch is "Teacher's Choice" selected from the five cards in your possession.

4. During each stretch, ask another volunteer to repeat the definition of good flexibility, or have the class repeat it in unison.

5. Rotate volunteers until all stretches are performed.

TEACHING HINTS

■ Adjust the number of cards used based on time available. Use other cards when revisiting the activity. Remove used cards after students perform the stretch; or if time allows, place used cards back in the box (or keep them in your possession) to be redrawn.

■ Circulate among students to encourage slow, sustained stretching and other aspects of safe stretching.

■ Discourage competition among students for how far each can push a stretch. Reinforce the need for each student to find his or her own point of mild discomfort and to back off slightly.

SAMPLE INCLUSION TIPS

■ Allow students with disabilities to perform activities prior to incorporating modifications.

■ The buddy system allows opportunity to work with others.

■ Use verbal and visual aids/picture cues as well as physical cues or demonstrations and allow students with disabilities to mirror peers.

■ Provide yoga-style stretching straps, or similar aids, to assist those students who have limited flexibility or find it difficult to get into the correct positions.

ASSESSMENT

At the end of class, ask each student to write the definition of good flexibility. Check written definitions to ensure that each student understands the key points, but allow students to use their own words.

5.2 All-Star Stretches

MIDDLE AND HIGH SCHOOL

Health benefits—Keeping your joints flexible is important in promoting overall health and safe participation in physical activity. Benefits of stretching include a maintained or increased range of motion; a decreased risk of injury in sports, daily chores, and tasks; increased blood supply and nutrients to the joints; reduced muscular soreness after activity; and improved balance, mobility, and posture.

PURPOSE

- Students will understand the benefits of good flexibility.
- Students will identify unsafe versus safe stretches and stretching practices.

RELATIONSHIP TO NATIONAL STANDARDS

Physical Education Standard 4: Achieves and maintains a health-enhancing level of physical fitness.

Physical Education Standard 5: Exhibits responsible personal and social behavior that respects self and others in physical activity settings.

Health Education Standard 1: Students will comprehend concepts related to health promotion and disease prevention.

EQUIPMENT

PROCEDURE

1. Explain that good flexibility can only be achieved through practicing safe stretching techniques. If you injure yourself stretching incorrectly, you will not benefit. Review the Guidelines for Safe Stretching Poster. Mention that certain types of stretches that students may have heard of or used, such as PNF and dynamic (ballistic) stretches are only for specific situations, such as sport training, and can be done safely only under carefully guided conditions. In this lesson, the focus will be on static and active stretching, as described on the poster.

2. Lead or have student leaders lead the class through a whole-body warm-up lasting three to five minutes (e.g., walking, then jogging in place, or a fast-paced review of dance steps).

3. Mix the Flexibility Task and Benefit and the Unsafe Stretching Risk cards together into a deck of cards and shuffle. Lead, or have student leaders lead, the class through each of the 16 cards. When a safe stretch comes up, read the health benefit written on the back of the card. When a practice that may be unsafe comes up, instead of performing it, read the reason for not performing it.

Reproducibles

- Flexibility Task and Benefit Cards (one set per group or for whole class)
- Unsafe Stretching Risk Cards
- Guidelines for Safe Stretching Poster
- Benefits of Good Flexibility Poster

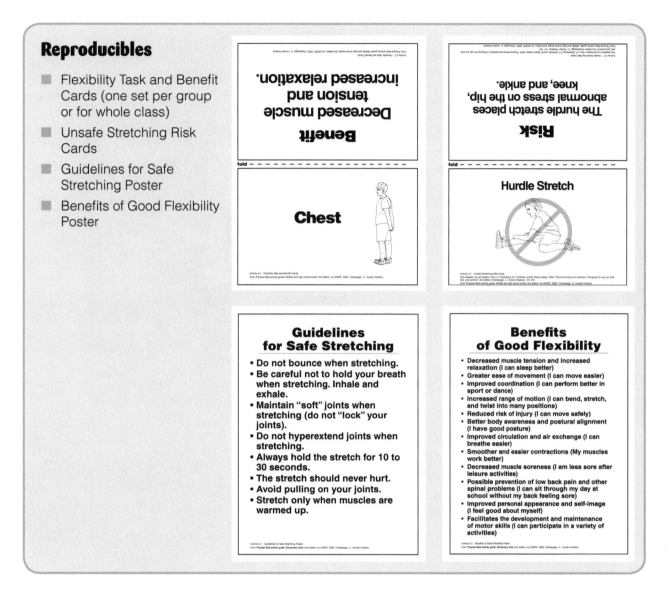

TEACHING HINTS

- To increase time on task for experienced students, eliminate step 1 under "Procedure" and simply hang the safety poster at each group's area to remind students of the safety guidelines.
- Connect the safety guidelines and benefits to the back-saver sit-and-reach test and shoulder stretch test in *FITNESSGRAM/ACTIVITYGRAM*.
- You may wish to point out that stretching to the point of mild discomfort and backing off slightly (but still feeling the stretch) applies the overload principle of training to flexibility.

SAMPLE INCLUSION TIPS

- As with the Flexibility Fling exercise, you can use towels, belts, neckties, lengths of clothesline, or rope as stretching straps. You can also use resistance bands.
- Some students with Down Syndrome will be prone to hyperflexibility (due to laxity in joint ligaments). Observe and also assign a peer buddy to observe the posture and alignment of the student with a disability during flexibility movements. Provide verbal and physical cues to produce correct movement.

ASSESSMENT

■ Have students name one or more benefits of good flexibility and relate those benefits to their everyday activities and/or sport activities in which they participate.

■ Offer a worksheet that shows three safe stretches and one unsafe practice. Ask students to identify the unsafe practice and to write or tell why it is unsafe.

5.3 Type Cast

MIDDLE AND HIGH SCHOOL

Specificity states that to increase flexibility of a particular area, a person must perform exercises for a specific muscle or muscle group, and must do it on a regular basis (flexibility exercises can be done daily). As stated in other chapters discussing the principles of training, each student should have individual goals based on need, physical limitations, or performance ambition.

PURPOSE

- Students will learn how to apply the principle of specificity in the area of flexibility.
- Students will identify specific muscle groups used in particular sports or activities.

RELATIONSHIP TO NATIONAL STANDARDS

Physical Education Standard 2: Demonstrates understanding of movement concepts, principles, strategies, and tactics as they apply to the learning and performance of physical activities.

Physical Education Standard 4: Achieves and maintains a health-enhancing level of physical fitness.

Physical Education Standard 5: Exhibits responsible personal and social behavior that respects self and others in physical activity settings.

EQUIPMENT

- Blank index cards, enough for one per group at each station
- Pencils, one per group
- Mats (optional)
- Relaxing background music and music player (optional)

PROCEDURE

1. Place flexibility stations around the activity area, each with one Flexibility Task and Benefit Card and several index cards.

2. As the class participates in a simple warm-up such as a brisk walk around the activity area, define and discuss flexibility. You may want to include the following points:

   - *Flexibility* is the ability to move a joint through its complete range of motion.

Reproducible

- Flexibility Task and Benefit Cards (use those provided on CD-ROM or supplement with additional cards of your own)

Benefit
Decreased muscle tension and increased relaxation

fold - - - - - - - - - - - - -

Chest

Activity 5.3 Flexibility Task and Benefit Cards
From *Physical Best activity guide: Middle and high school levels*, 2nd edition, by NASPE, 2005, Champaign, IL: Human Kinetics.

- A safe way to improve flexibility is to use static stretching: A static stretch is a slow, sustained stretch of the muscle.

- Stretch to the point of mild discomfort, then back off slightly and hold the stretch for 10 to 30 seconds. (Or you can hold the stretch at a point just before it becomes uncomfortable.)

- Identify the relationship between flexibility exercises and the ability to participate safely in physical activities.

- Explain that flexibility exercises are used after a warm-up to prepare the body for physical activity and after cool-down to further develop flexibility.

- Review with students the difference between warm-up and stretching. Warm-up is a low-level, nonstressful activity that uses the whole body for the purpose of stimulating the blood flow throughout the body. Warm-up is different from stretching. Stretching comes *after* warm-up and *after* cool-down. This is important because students may think that stretching *is* a warm-up and cool-down. Too often students begin group stretching without a moment's warm-up. This is not conducive to obtaining a good stretch and can actually lead to injury.

3. Remind students that flexibility is specific to the muscle group worked. That is, to gain flexible leg muscles, you have to perform stretches that stretch the leg joints and muscles; to gain flexible shoulders, you have to stretch the shoulder joint muscles. Point out that different activities—such as soccer, dance, and swimming—require flexibility in different parts of the body.

4. Divide students into groups of three or four students per group, give each group a pencil, and send each group to a station.

5. Instruct students to
   - perform the static stretch that appears on the Flexibility Task and Benefit Card for 10 to 30 seconds,
   - determine an appropriate activity that would benefit from this stretch (e.g., guarding in soccer, leaping in dance, arm strokes in swimming, etc.),
   - write that activity on a blank index card, and
   - leave both the index card (face down) and the Flexibility Task and Benefit Card at the station.

6. Rotate groups to new stations every couple of minutes, based on the amount of time available and number of stations. Stopping and starting music may help make the transition easier.

TEACHING HINTS

■ If needed, prior to commencing the activity, review the location and function of each muscle group that students are stretching as well as correct stretching form.

■ Set up enough stations to keep each group at four or fewer students. Make second copies of some of the cards, if needed.

■ Use flexibility stations after a warm-up or cool-down.

SAMPLE INCLUSION TIPS

■ Use peer assistants to demonstrate the proper technique for each stretch.

■ Allow students with disabilities to attempt to perform activities prior to incorporating modifications.

■ Tape arrows on the wall or floor to direct students to the next station.

ASSESSMENT

■ Collect all index cards with students' activity suggestions written on them. As a class, review and evaluate students' selection of activities for several flexibility stations.

■ As a whole class, have students name the muscle group(s) stretched at each station.

5.4 Sport Spectacular

HIGH SCHOOL

Specificity states that to increase flexibility of a particular area, a person must perform exercises for a specific muscle or muscle group, and must do it on a regular basis (flexibility exercises can be done daily). As stated in other chapters discussing the principles of training, each student should have individual goals based on need, physical limitations, or performance ambition.

PURPOSE

- Students will explore specific stretches for a physical activity or sport in which they are interested.
- Students will enhance their flexibility through participating in sport- or activity-specific stretches over time and connect the principle of type (specificity) to the benefits of injury prevention and enhanced performance.

RELATIONSHIP TO NATIONAL STANDARDS

Physical Education Standard 3: Participates regularly in physical activity.

Physical Education Standard 4: Achieves and maintains a health-enhancing level of physical fitness.

Health Education Standard 1: Students will comprehend concepts related to health promotion and disease prevention.

EQUIPMENT

- Mats (optional)
- Blank sheets of paper for self-designed specific flexibility workout pages (optional)
- 1 sign per sport or activity to mark stations where related reproducible can be found (optional)
- Pencils

PROCEDURE

1. Review or teach students the principle of specificity. Briefly discuss how it applies to flexibility training.

2. Give an overview of the sports and activities for which you have flexibility training workout sheets to offer. Ask students to select one sport or activity to work on flexibility today.

3. Lead, or have student leaders lead, a whole-body warm-up for a minimum of five minutes (an aerobic fitness activity is preferable).

Reproducible

- Sport Stretch Pages, one per student or one per group

4. Divide class into four groups and send each group to one of the activity areas to practice the stretches shown on the related sheet. Require students to repeat the stretches according to safety guidelines as time allows. Have students fill in the "muscles and body part(s) stretched" section individually or as a group.

5. Gather students back into the main group to briefly discuss how they predict that the specific stretches might enhance their sport performance, if performed frequently enough with appropriate intensity.

© Human Kinetics

TEACHING HINTS

■ If a student is not interested in one of the sports or activities offered in the reproducibles, help that student choose appropriate stretches from other sources, for another sport or activity. In other words, choose wisely to create a specific flexibility-training workout that will enhance performance in the preferred sport or activity.

■ If possible, have students follow their sport- or activity-specific stretching with the sport or activity itself, both in and outside of class, and end it with a cool-down that includes some or all of the sport- or activity-specific stretches.

■ Over multiple class sessions, have students switch to different activity areas until all four Sport Stretch Pages are completed.

SAMPLE INCLUSION TIPS

■ Allow students with disabilities to attempt to perform activities prior to incorporating modifications.

■ The buddy system allows all students the opportunity to work with others. Use verbal and visual aids/picture cues as well as physical cues or demonstrations and allow students with disabilities to mirror peers.

ASSESSMENT

■ Discuss the "muscles and body parts stretched" section for each sport and stretch.

■ Require students to log their sport- or activity-specific flexibility training over the course of one to four weeks. Ask students to write comments as to how specificity in flexibility training may help them enhance their performance in the sport or activity.

5.5 Introduction to Yoga

MIDDLE AND HIGH SCHOOL

The recommended **frequency** for flexibility training is daily (three times per week minimum but preferably daily) to attain the maximum benefits. **Time** refers to how long the stretch is held, and there is a wide variety of suggestions ranging from 10 seconds through 1 minute. The American College of Sports Medicine (2000) proposes a stretch be held 10 to 30 seconds. (Note that a student should always begin holding a stretch for a short period of time and gradually progress to the 30-second time period.)

PURPOSE

- Students will learn to apply the frequency and time components of the FITT Guidelines to flexibility through an introduction to yoga.
- Students will learn a flexibility activity that can reduce stress and increase relaxation.

RELATIONSHIP TO NATIONAL STANDARDS

Physical Education Standard 6: Values physical activity for health, enjoyment, challenge, self-expression and/or social interaction.

Health Education Standard 3: Students will demonstrate the ability to practice health-enhancing behaviors and reduce health risks.

EQUIPMENT

- Mats
- Relaxing music

PROCEDURE

1. Place mats and the laminated Yoga Signs at stations throughout the activity area (or use your own cards if you prefer). Lights should be dim, and relaxing music should be playing as students enter.

2. To introduce the activity, explain the procedure to students during the class period before this activity. Ask them to remember to enter the class setting quietly. You might briefly discuss yoga, its benefits, its history, and so on. In addition, mention how yoga can reduce stress and increase feelings of relaxation.

3. Have students perform a light warm-up, such as walking for a few minutes.

4. After brief instructions, have students remove their shoes and choose a station. Remind students to be quiet. Have students face you, and lead them in the mountain pose as a group. While this pose is not a stretch, it is an opportunity to set the tone for the activity. Following that, have the students read the card and look at the picture, then attempt the yoga position.

5. Allow about two minutes for reading and practicing, then turn the music down as a signal to move to the next station.

6. Allow students to go through as many stations as you desire, or as time permits. Finish with the final relaxation pose as a group.

Reproducibles

- Yoga Signs, laminated
- Yoga Pose Cards, one per student, copied, two pages or double sided
- Yoga Log, one per student

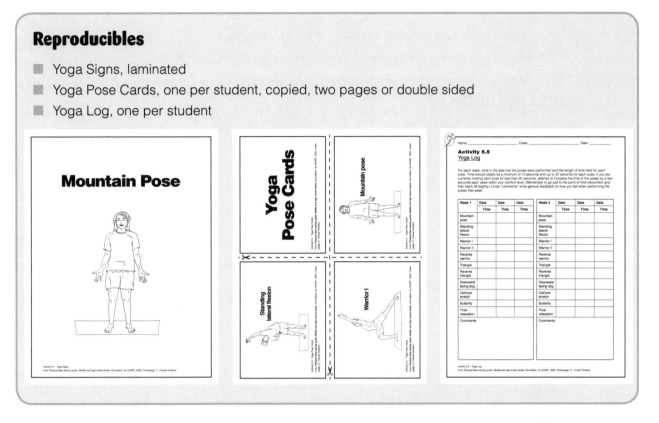

7. Pass out the Yoga Pose Cards and Yoga Logs and ask students to practice the poses three times per week when their muscles are warmed up. Discuss time in relation to flexibility and ask them to log their frequency and time on their log for the next two to four weeks.

TEACHING HINTS

- Familiarize yourself and students with yoga poses and related safety information before teaching this activity.

- Before the lesson, design a bulletin board display of yoga pictures and basic information, including its relationship to athletic performance (and overall wellness).

- Use available yoga videos that students can easily follow once they have practiced. Some videos even combine yoga with power and endurance moves for very challenging workouts. We recommend Beth Shaw's *YogaFit* (2001) book and video as references for this activity. For more information on *YogaFit*, visit www.yogafit.com or call Human Kinetics at 800-747-4457 to order copies. The video is about 30 minutes long, which is a good length for school classes.

▦ Have students design their own yoga routine, using the poses—starting with the mountain pose and finishing with the final relaxation pose.

▦ Note that some poses will need to be performed on the right and left side of the body.

SAMPLE INCLUSION TIP

For students with a cognitive/learning disability or those with a behavioral/emotional disorder, use the peer buddy system. You can also circulate the room, providing assistance as needed.

ASSESSMENT

▦ After the two to four week period, collect logs and lead a class discussion on the logs. Additional discussion suggestions:

• What does the student think was the most challenging aspect of this activity?

• Have the student describe why yoga can reduce stress.

• How might the student incorporate yoga into an overall fitness plan?

Body Composition

Chapter Contents

- Body Composition, Physical Activity, and Nutrition

- Teaching Guidelines for Body Composition

- Activities

© Human Kinetics

The activities in this chapter explore body composition, an important component of fitness. At the middle and high school levels, students should understand the major concepts regarding body composition:

■ Energy intake and expenditure
■ Guidelines for healthy eating such as the Food Guide Pyramid
■ Factors that affect body composition such as genetics, diet, and physical activity

When completing these activities, students should understand how their behaviors will affect their body composition. The following information introduces the subject of body composition at the middle and high school levels. For more information on this topic, refer to *Physical Education for Lifelong Fitness: The Physical Best Teacher's Guide, Second Edition*, chapters 4 and 8, which focus on nutrition and body composition.

Body Composition, Physical Activity, and Nutrition

Body composition is the amount of lean body mass (all tissues other than fat, such as bone, muscle, organs, and body fluids) compared with the amount of body fat, usually expressed in terms of percent body fat. Among the common ways to assess whether body composition is appropriate are BMI-for-age tables, skinfold caliper testing, height-weight tables, and waist-to-hip ratio.

As with any other component of health-related fitness, a person's body composition does not develop in isolation from the other components. Indeed, you should show students the connections among all health-related fitness components so that they can see how their personal choices affect this area of health-related fitness. Although genetics, environment, and culture play significant roles, body composition results largely from physical activity levels in the other components:

■ **aerobic fitness**—Aerobic activities expend calories.

■ **muscular strength and endurance**—Muscle cells expend (metabolize) more calories at rest than fat cells do. To increase the likelihood that students will maintain appropriate body composition, emphasize physical activity that follows the principles of training.

■ **flexibility**—A flexible body can better tolerate aerobic fitness and muscular strength and endurance activities.

Of course, nutrition also plays an important role in body composition. In addition to reviewing the Food Guide Pyramid (see reproducible on CD-ROM for activity 6.7, Health Quest), discuss appropriate portion sizes. In the United States, portion sizes have been increasing for the last three decades. The Western diet includes many highly processed, high-fat, high-sugar, and high-salt foods. The human body was designed to work best with whole grains, vegetables, and fruits.

Nutrients fall into six classes: carbohydrates, protein, fat, vitamins, minerals, and water. Because all nutrients are essential for good health, the diet must contain all six.

■ Carbohydrates provide most of the energy for people across the world and represent the preferred source of energy for the body. People should obtain carbohydrates from whole grains, cereals, vegetables, and fruits. Refined grains and sugars can also provide carbohydrates.

- Protein serves as the structural component for vital body parts. Every cell in the body contains protein. In the United States, meat is the primary source of protein.

- Fat serves as a concentrated form of energy, and the human body stores excess calories as fat.

- Vitamins and minerals contain no calories, but small amounts are essential for good health.

- Many students do not realize that water is an essential nutrient. Students need to drink at least six to eight cups of water daily.

Teaching Guidelines for Body Composition

Approach discussions about body composition objectively and as a topic about which students should be sensitive. Strive to point out connections among physical activity, nutrition, and body composition related to daily life, recreational activities, and physical education activities. Never use a student as a positive or negative example regarding body composition. Heavier students may become uncomfortable, so be prepared to help them approach this as a learning process, not as a negative or punitive message. Emphasize that a student who is overfat because of genetics can still greatly reduce health risks by being physically active. Remember, students will follow your lead with their peers. If you're comfortable with the topic, they will be too.

Society places a great deal of emphasis on physical appearance, and this attention to appearance becomes very important during puberty. As a physical educator, you must help students find satisfaction with their appearance rather than try to measure up to cultural expectations. When exploring this topic, you may encounter students who are below or above normal ranges for body composition or who have diagnosed or undiagnosed eating disorders, such as the following:

- Anorexia nervosa—characterized by extremely low caloric intake with a distorted body image.
- Bulimia nervosa—characterized by large food binges followed by purging with vomiting or laxatives.
- Binge-eating disorder—characterized by large food binges with no compensatory behavior. This results, of course, in periods of rapid weight gain.

Be on the lookout for warning signs of each eating disorder. If you suspect an eating disorder, be sure to discuss this with the school nurse, school dietitian, and principal before deciding how to proceed.

Although approaching body composition in the physical education setting can be a delicate matter, it's an important component of fitness and must be addressed. Handle body composition instruction professionally by concentrating on how a healthy diet and active lifestyle can positively affect it. Encourage a positive self-image and emphasize that normal bodies comes in all sizes.

Activities

Chapter 6 Activities Grid

Activity number	Activity title	Activity page	Concept	Middle school	High school	Reproducible (on CD-Rom)
6.1	Build a Body	**107**	Definition	●		None
6.2	All Sport Body Comp Quizzo	**110**	Definition	●	●	Body Composition Quizzo Chart
						Body Composition Quizzo Term Cards
						All Sport Body Composition Activity List
6.3	Body Comp Survivor	**113**	Health benefits	●	●	Body Composition Survivor Challenges
						Three Body Composition Puzzles
						Super Survivor Questions
6.4	Frisbee Calorie Blaster	**117**	Health benefits		●	None
6.5	1,000 Reps	**119**	Growth and development	●		1,000 Reps and Seconds Chart
						Estimated Energy Expenditure for Common Activities Chart
6.6	Cross-Training Triumph	**122**	Growth and development		●	Cross-Training Triumph Task Cards
6.7	Health Quest	**125**	Nutrition	●	●	Checkpoint Signs
						Health Quest Answer Sheets
						Food Guide Pyramid
6.8	Fast Food Frenzy	**128**	Nutrition	●	●	Fast Food Frenzy Discovery Worksheet
						Calorie Chart
						Instructions for Stations 1 to 7
						Lunch Menu Suggestion Cards
						Health Behavior Contract
6.9	Mass Metabolism	**133**	Metabolism and nutrition	●		My Metabolism Log

6.1 Build a Body

MIDDLE SCHOOL

Body composition is the amount of body fat as compared to the amount of lean body mass (all tissues other than fat, such as bone, muscle, organs, and body fluids), usually expressed in terms of percent body fat. Healthy body composition (ratio of fat to lean weight) and adequate hydration are key factors for disease prevention and health.

PURPOSE

- Students will be able to define body composition.
- Students will be able to recognize a healthy balance of fat and lean body mass.
- Students will learn the great need the body has for water because fluid comprises over half of one's body weight.

RELATIONSHIP TO NATIONAL STANDARDS

Physical Education Standard 4: Achieves and maintains a health-enhancing level of physical fitness.

Physical Education Standard 5: Exhibits responsible personal and social behavior that respects self and others in physical activity settings.

Health Education Standard 1: Students will comprehend concepts related to health promotion and disease prevention.

EQUIPMENT

- Hula hoops, three hoops plus one additional hoop for every four students
- Gray balls or any object that represents fat, approximately 20, or at least two balls for every four students
- Blue balls or any object that represents fluid, approximately 60, or at least six balls for every four students
- Red balls or any object that represents lean body tissue, approximately 20, or at least two balls for every four students
- Picture of an extremely thin person (if using second assessment idea), preferably a currently popular famous person from a magazine, newspaper, or the Internet

PROCEDURE

1. Set up three hula hoops in the middle of the gym. Fill one hoop up with the object that represents fat, one hoop with the object that represents water, and one hoop with the object that represents lean body tissue (aside from fluids).

2. Spread the rest of the hoops in a large circle around the three middle hoops.

3. Explain to the students the definition of body composition, and that the body needs some amount of fat to function normally. For instance, the body gets energy for some types of physical activity from fat. There is a range of "normal" for body fat

Reproducible

- none

percentage. Explain that this is a personal issue and that heredity and cultural influences can be a factor in body composition. The body fat ranges for students recommended by Physical Best and FITNESSGRAM are 10 to 25 percent for males and 17 to 32 percent for females. Tell students that everybody's body is slightly different, but for the activity today, to use the estimate that fluids make up approximately 60 percent of body mass, and the rest of the lean tissue makes up approximately 20 percent of body mass. That leaves a medium point in the recommended ranges of about 20 percent for fat. Explain that with these percentages, it is easy to tell that the body needs a large amount of water to function well, so drinking a lot of water makes sense.

4. Divide the class into groups with roughly four students in a group, and send each group to one of the empty hoops around the activity area.

5. Explain that each group must strive to build a body with two fat objects, six fluid objects, and two lean body objects.

6. One at a time, a member of a group may leave the team's hoop area to bring an object to the team's hoop or discard an object from the team's hoop. Tell students to choose a sequence, so that they know which team member they follow and can move into action quickly. Students can only carry one object at a time. They can run, but they must carefully place balls in the hula hoops (they can't throw or toss the balls).

7. Team members may take objects from other groups to get the right body proportions for their team, or they may give other teams objects to upset the proportions that those teams have acquired. Students may not block their hula hoops from other teams or push other students out of the way.

8. Because regular physical activity contributes to healthy body composition, when a member of a team is not taking a turn to find or discard a ball, have him or her

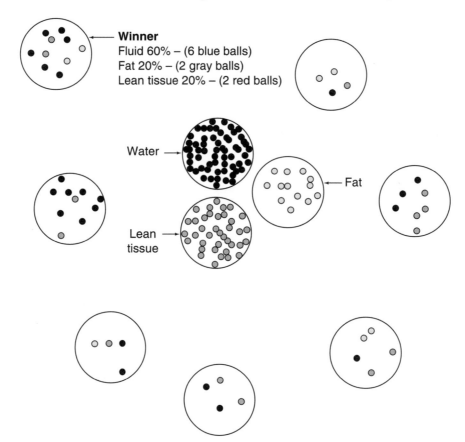

Winner
Fluid 60% – (6 blue balls)
Fat 20% – (2 gray balls)
Lean tissue 20% – (2 red balls)

Water

Fat

Lean tissue

choose one of three activities that you specify (pick one muscular strength, one muscular endurance, and one flexibility activity) and rotate with each turn. Another option is to have nonactive team members working together on strategies.

9. When a team has two fats, six fluids, and two lean objects they should sit around their hoop and put their arms up to let the teacher know that they were successful.

TEACHING HINTS

- Add more objects to the hoops to make the game easier; use fewer objects to make the game more difficult.

- Alter the number of hoops and objects to fit class size.

- Consider not allowing any running, and offer an alternative locomotor if running would be unsafe in your situation. Penalize teams who break rules regarding running, blocking, or shoving.

- Alter the activity by placing objects that represent the proportion of food servings in the Food Guide Pyramid in the hoops, to give the students information on nutrition.

- To use this activity as a warm-up, do not allow running and have students who are not taking a turn march in place. If using this activity as the main workout, include a warm-up, such as walking around the perimeter of the playing area, before progressing to the activity.

SAMPLE INCLUSION TIPS

- For students with a cognitive/learning disability, use both verbal and picture cues to help students know what their hoop should contain at the end of the game.

- For students with visual disabilities, who are often not exposed or provided opportunities to engage in moderate aerobic activity, thus have tendencies to become overweight/obese individuals; use a different shaped ball that represents each of the components: fat (largest ball, i.e., a beach ball or balloon), lean body mass (smallest of balls, perhaps a tennis ball that when bounced would simulate action of muscle tissue), and fluids (textured balls, especially ones that can have fluid placed in the inside). The student can then feel each ball and with a sighted guide engage in activity by carrying balls to designated spots.

ASSESSMENT

- Verbally quiz students:
  - Why is it important to drink a lot of water?
  - Does the body need fat? What are its purposes for body functioning?
  - How do you promote healthy lean body mass?

- Find a picture from a publication showing a famous person who is extremely thin. Then have each student write a paragraph about why pictures like these might have a negative effect on young people. (Be sure to point out that being thin is not wrong. Some people are naturally very thin. It's when a person takes extreme measures to be thin that we become concerned.)

- As a homework assignment, have students find one site on the Internet that talks about body composition, and have them bring a printout or a handwritten URL to prove that they did this. (If you have students with limited access to the Internet, give the class at least a week to complete this assignment.) Discuss the information the students found, reinforcing the learning.

6.2 All Sport Body Comp Quizzo

MIDDLE AND HIGH SCHOOL

Body composition is the amount of body fat compared to the amount of lean body mass (all tissues other than fat, such as bone, muscle, organs, and body fluids), usually expressed in terms of percentage of body fat.

PURPOSE

- Students will review a variety of body composition terms while engaging in physical activity.
- Students will match the body composition term to its corresponding definition.

RELATIONSHIP TO NATIONAL STANDARDS

Physical Education Standard 4: Achieves and maintains a health-enhancing level of physical fitness.

Health Education Standard 1: Students will comprehend concepts related to health promotion and disease prevention.

EQUIPMENT

- Basketballs, one per group
- Volleyballs, one per group
- Jump ropes, one per group

Reproducibles

- Body Composition Quizzo Chart (one for each group)
- Body Composition Quizzo Term Cards (one set for each group)
- All Sport Body Composition Activity List (one for each group)

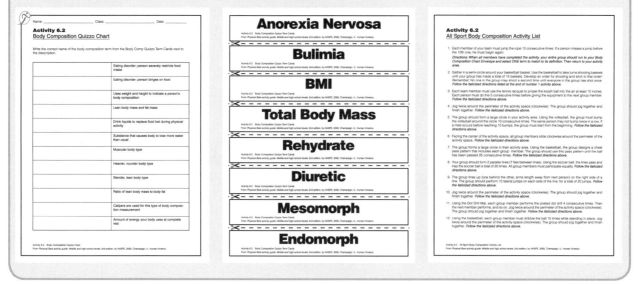

- Tennis rackets and koosh balls, one per group
- Soccer balls, one per group
- Dot Drill Mat (or dots taped to the floor)
- Laminated envelope
- Pencils

PROCEDURE

1. Before class begins, post each group's Body Composition Quizzo Chart in a separate area of the activity space; evenly space these charts.

2. Next to each chart, post an envelope that contains all of the Body Composition Quizzo Term Cards.

3. Ask students to explain the relationship between body composition and physical activity.

4. Explain that today's lesson will combine physical activity with a body composition term review.

5. Ask students to name a few body composition terms (metabolism, and so on).

6. Discuss the activity guidelines:

- Each group works cooperatively as a team to accomplish specific tasks and earn term cards. Once a team has earned a term card, they must report it on their Body Composition Quizzo Chart by writing the term next to the correct description.

- Once they have matched a term correctly, the team may begin the next activity on their list. After completing each separate activity (in order) on the list, the team may select one more term from the envelope to match to its definition on their Body Composition Quizzo Chart.

- The ultimate goal is for each group to match all of the term cards to the correct definitions on their Body Composition Quizzo Chart. But remind them that the group can earn only *one* term card for each completed activity. To earn another term card, the group must complete the next activity.

- Divide students into groups of four to six students per group.

- Give each group an All Sport Body Composition Activity List. Then assign each group to a specific area of the gymnasium where they will find the equipment necessary to complete the activities.
- When a group has completed all activities, and thereby matched all terms to their appropriate definitions, ask the group to double-check their answers.

TEACHING HINTS

- Modify the All Sport Body Composition Activity List to meet the interests of your students or your equipment inventory.
- To use the activity repeatedly, and/or with other classes, laminate each of the reproducible items, and place Velcro on the backs of the Term Cards and on the blanks on the Quizzo Chart.
- The Body Composition Quizzo Term Cards are in the correct order (reading from left to right) to match the Body Composition Quizzo Chart. You will want to shuffle the cards for the students' use, but can refer to the original printout of the cards as an answer key.

SAMPLE INCLUSION TIPS

- For classes that have students with a cognitive/learning disability, assign a group leader to read aloud, interpret the activities, and guide the group in performing the activities.
- For students with physical impairments, modify the activities as needed. For example, split jump ropes, lower the basketball hoop, and so on.

ASSESSMENT

When all groups are finished, ask students to assemble in front of one particular group's Body Composition Chart. Ask the following questions:

- Which was the easiest term to match? Why?
- Which term was most challenging to match? Why?
- How can the activities you completed today affect your individual body composition?
- How would you explain body composition to an elementary-aged student?

6.3 Body Comp Survivor (a.k.a. BC Survivor)

MIDDLE/HIGH SCHOOL

Health benefits—Achieving and maintaining a healthy body composition can reduce one's risk for many diseases, and offers many benefits such as increased self-esteem and energy level.

PURPOSE

Students will participate in an activity that teaches the benefits of healthy body composition, risks associated with a high percentage of body fat, and many other facts related to body composition.

RELATIONSHIP TO NATIONAL STANDARDS

Physical Education Standard 4: Achieves and maintains a health-enhancing level of physical fitness.

Physical Education Standard 5: Exhibits responsible personal and social behavior that respects self and others in physical activity settings.

Health Education Standard 1: Students will comprehend concepts related to health promotion and disease prevention.

EQUIPMENT

- Red, blue, and yellow cardstock
- Quart-sized plastic bags, one for each group; bag contains all of that group's puzzle pieces
- Pencils
- Koosh balls, one per team
- Inflated balloons, three per 4-person team
- 4 inch by 4-inch tarps, one per team
- 12 inch by 12-inch carpet square
- 3 beanbags per team
- 1 small bucket per team
- Red floor tape (to mark spot for each tribe's bucket and the line 10 feet from bucket)
- 2 poly spots per group

PROCEDURE

Advance preparations:

1. Print the Benefits of Developing and Maintaining Ideal Body Composition sheet onto 8 1/2 x 11 inch red cardstock. Print the Risk of Having High Percentage of Body Fat sheet onto blue cardstock. Print the Body Composition Facts sheet onto yellow cardstock. Print a copy of each sheet for every four students (number of students per tribe) in your class.

Reproducibles

■ Body Composition Survivor Challenges

■ The three Body Composition Puzzles

- Benefits of Developing and Maintaining Ideal Body Composition Puzzle

- Risks of Having a High Percentage of Body Fat Puzzle

- Body Composition Facts Puzzle

■ Super Survivor Questions

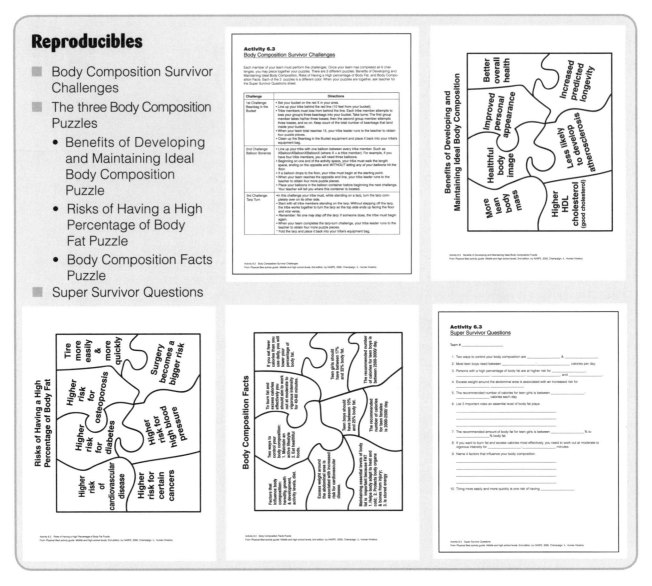

2. Cut each sheet of cardstock into individual puzzle pieces. Place puzzle pieces for each group in a quart-size plastic bag. Use a permanent marker to number each of the bags (1–6, if you have six bags).

3. Give a copy of the Body Composition Survivor Challenges to each group of four, or tribe. Make the same number of copies of the Super Survivor Questions to pass out later.

4. To accommodate the "Beanbag in the Bucket" Challenge, tape a red "X" on the floor and tape a red line 10 feet from the "X" using the red floor tape. Do this in each group's designated area.

5. Place each group's equipment in a giant trash bag. Each group needs: 1 Koosh ball, 4 balloons, 1 tarp, 3 beanbags, 1 small bucket, and 3 poly spots. Put this bag in each tribe's designated area.

During class:

1. Explain that the class will be competing in a new game show: Body Comp Survivor, a.k.a. BC Survivor. The class will be divided into tribes of four, which will compete in challenges to earn pieces of the three different puzzles. Each tribe will have a tribe number, which is the number printed on that tribe's quart-sized plastic bag of puzzle pieces. (Teacher keeps these bags.) The completed puzzles will

outline important body composition information that the tribes will need to complete the Super Survivor Questions. The ultimate challenge is to be the first tribe to put together all three of the puzzles and correctly answer the Super Survivor Questions. That team will win the coveted Super Survivor Champs Award.

2. Designate a specific spot of the activity area for each tribe. Each tribe's equipment bag should be placed in this area. (Note to teacher: Be certain you have taped on the floor the red "X" and red line for each tribe's "Beanbag in the Bucket" Challenge.)

3. Emphasize that the tribe members must work cooperatively to accomplish their challenges. Once a tribe has completed a challenge, the tribe leader must report to the teacher, who will give the leader four puzzle pieces from that tribe's plastic bag. (Tribe leader must state his/her tribe's number before receiving puzzle pieces from the teacher.) This process will be repeated after a tribe successfully completes each challenge (on the Body Composition Survivor Challenges).

4. When a tribe has accumulated all puzzle pieces, they piece together each puzzle. When a tribe has put together all three puzzles, the leader reports to the teacher who will provide the Super Survivor Questions and a pencil. Note: The only way a tribe can have all puzzle pieces is if they have finished all six Survivor Challenges.

5. The first tribe to answer correctly all of the questions on the Super Survivor Question Sheet wins the title of Super Survivor Champs.

TEACHING HINTS

■ During the introduction to the activity, play a tape of the theme music from the *Survivor* television show.

■ Divide tribes into heterogeneous groups.

■ Laminate the puzzle pieces to preserve them.

■ Design an outrageously fun award for the winning team: small trophy with plastic flower decorations or Mardi Gras beads for each winner with a big laminated cardstock medal that states: BC Survivor Champ.

SAMPLE INCLUSION TIP

For classes that have students with a cognitive/learning disability, assign a group leader to read aloud, interpret the activities, and guide the group in performing the activities.

ASSESSMENT

- At the conclusion of the activity, gather all tribes in a central location to process the body composition information:
  - What fact surprised you the most? Why?
  - What fact would you most want to share with your parent or guardian? Why?
  - Which fact do you believe teenagers most need to know? Why?
  - What are the benefits of maintaining ideal body composition?
- To extend the activity, have each tribe design a poster or write a paragraph that summarizes the body composition concepts learned during the BC Survivor game.

6.4 Frisbee Calorie Blaster

HIGH SCHOOL

Health benefits—*Body composition* is the amount of body fat compared to the amount of lean body mass (all tissues other than fat, such as bone, muscle, organs, and body fluids), usually expressed in terms of percentage of body fat. Although genetics plays a role, to a large extent a *healthy body composition* can be obtained and maintained through a balance of regular physical activity and moderate calorie intake. Having a *healthy body composition* leads to many health benefits, including a healthier cardio-vascular system, lower risk of diabetes, increased self-esteem, less strain on joints, and having more energy.

PURPOSE

- Students will learn that reducing or expending 500 more calories a day than one needs to maintain weight will result in a one-pound weight loss over a week.
- Students will see that physical activity can be fun and that physical activity helps expend calories, leading to healthy body composition.

RELATIONSHIP TO NATIONAL STANDARDS

Physical Education Standard 4: Achieves and maintains a health-enhancing level of physical fitness.

Health Education Standard 1: Students will comprehend concepts related to health promotion and disease prevention.

EQUIPMENT

- Small Frisbees, two per student
- 14 plastic bowling pins
- Floor tape or poly spots (optional) to mark the playing zones

PROCEDURE

1. Set up seven pins at each end of the activity space, 5 to 10 feet from the wall (see diagram). Spread the pins evenly across the width of the space. Establish an area of four to six feet in front of the pins as the "neutral zone," where no one may enter for the purpose of defense (guarding the pins). Mark a midcourt, or center, line. Floor tape or poly spots can be used if lines on the floor are not available.

2. Discuss with the class that for individuals who wish or need to improve body composition, moderate and consistent changes in diet and activity level will result in positive changes in body composition. Having a healthy body composition can lead to many health benefits, including a healthier cardiovascular system, lower risk of diabetes, increased self-esteem, less strain on joints, and more energy.

3. Teach the rules of the game. Explain that the objective is to knock down the opposing team's pins by *sliding the Frisbees across the floor* before they eliminate your pins. In today's activity, each pin represents 500 calories. By knocking down,

Reproducible

- none

or eliminating, all seven pins, students will eliminate one pound of body weight (3,500 calories). Students cannot cross the mid-court line at any time. Students must play offense, defend their pins, and retrieve Frisbees in order to be successful.

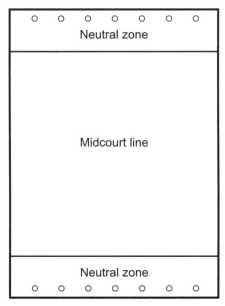

4. Have students practice the "Frisbee slide," sliding their Frisbees skillfully and safely.

5. Divide the students into two teams. Have students scatter randomly in their half of the playing area. Evenly distribute Frisbees to each team. Have team members decide who will slide the Frisbees toward the other team's pins, and who will guard their pins. Defenders may retrieve Frisbees, but may not enter the neutral zone.

6. On your signal, students begin the game (and expend those calories!).

7. This activity requires quite a bit of movement. You can play until one team has eliminated the other team's pins or for a set period of time. Teams set up the pins and switch sides for additional rounds.

8. Play as many rounds as desired.

TEACHING HINTS

- Once students learn the game, play upbeat music in the background.

- In large classes split teams into three groups—throwers (along midcourt), defenders (in front of the neutral zone), and retrievers (behind pins along each end wall; they must pass the Frisbees up to the throwers). Have each group wear different color pinnies and rotate each round. Although this minimizes overall movement, it may prove safer for large groups, and it emphasizes the strategies necessary for success.

SAMPLE INCLUSION TIPS

- A student with a disability can be provided with different types of objects that are safe to roll or toss, but may be easier to grip and manipulate.

- Incorporating appropriate safety techniques, students with disabilities could be allowed to move closer for more opportunity to throw and knock down pins.

ASSESSMENT

- Ask students to name some activities they enjoy doing that they think expend calories and promote healthy body composition. Ask how they could realistically reduce the amount of calories consumed on a daily basis if they needed to improve their body composition. (Point out that not everyone should reduce the number of calories consumed. A person of below-normal body composition should not try to lose weight.)

- Have students design a one-week plan that reduces 3,500 calories through a combination of reduced calorie intake and increased activity level. (They should use calorie charts or food labels, and determine calorie expenditure for chosen activities.) Consider having students who should maintain or gain weight design a one-week plan to maintain their weight or to add calories through healthy eating while participating in regular physical activity.

6.5

1,000 Reps

MIDDLE SCHOOL

Growth and development—A healthy body composition relies on *energy balance*, that is, a balance of "energy in" (calories eaten) and "energy out" (calories expended through metabolism and physical activity).

PURPOSE

- Students will be able to explain the relationship among diet, physical activity, and body composition.
- Students will be instructed on how physical activity can impact growth and development.
- Students will summarize how both diet and physical activity are important for maintaining optimum health.

RELATIONSHIP TO NATIONAL STANDARDS

Physical Education Standard 4: Achieves and maintains a health-enhancing level of physical fitness.

Health Education Standard 1: Student will comprehend concepts related to health promotion and disease prevention.

EQUIPMENT

- Pencils, one per student
- Other equipment will vary according to stations selected but could include:
  - jump ropes
  - resistance bands or dumbbells
  - basketballs and hoop

Reproducibles

- 1,000 Reps and Seconds Chart, one per student
- Estimated Energy Expenditure for Common Activities Chart, one per student

- soccer balls and cones for goals
- aerobic step benches
- tennis rackets and balls
- 6 mats
- TV, VCR, or DVD player, and cardio-kickboxing tape

PROCEDURE

1. Set up 10 to 12 stations: Some are timed activities and some require repetitions. The following are some suggestions:
- Jump ropes—number of jumps in two minutes
- Line dance—number of seconds
- A resistance band or dumbbells for chest presses—number of presses (use weight training on energy expenditure chart)
- A jogging area—number of seconds jogged
- Walking—number of seconds
- Basketballs and hoop—number baskets attempted
- Soccer balls and cones—number of goals attempted
- Aerobic steps—number of seconds
- Push-up station—number of push-ups completed (use fitness calisthenics on energy expenditure chart)
- Curl-up station—number of curl-ups completed (use fitness calisthenics on energy expenditure chart)
- Tennis—number of hits off a wall
- Cardio-kickboxing—number of seconds (use dance, aerobic on energy expenditure chart)

2. Explain to students that physical activity (a) expends calories for the energy used by the activity, (b) requires the body to use nutrients to maintain existing muscle tissue, and (c) requires the body to use nutrients to build new muscle tissue, therefore contributing to the body's healthy growth and development.

© Human Kinetics

3. After a proper warm-up, distribute a 1,000 Reps and Seconds Chart and a pencil to each student. Divide students into small groups of two to three, depending on the number of students and stations, and direct students to their stations.

4. Explain that students will use the charts to record the number of repetitions or the number of seconds for the activity at each station. At skills-based stations (such as basketball shooting), ask students to count the number of attempts, not the number of successes, because the goal is activity rather than performance. For timed activities, students need to count total time. For instance, if a student jumps rope for 20 seconds, then after a brief break for 20 more seconds, she would record a score of 40 for that station.

5. Direct students to move clockwise to the next station every two minutes. The objective is to reach at least 1,000 at the end of the class session by adding seconds (for timed activities) and repetitions (for repeated activities).

TEACHING HINTS

■ The most effective approach to this activity is using partners (two students per station).

■ Make and post interesting facts at each of the stations such as these: Muscle (lean tissue) weighs *more* than fat for equal volume. You must have a certain amount of fat to be healthy: Fat helps your body use vitamins, insulates your body, and protects your bones and body organs (Corbin and Lindsey 2004).

■ When revisiting this activity, change some of the stations to coordinate with the rest of your curriculum and to maintain interest. Use the second assessment idea to save time while reinforcing the learning.

SAMPLE INCLUSION TIPS

■ Supply calculators for students who will have trouble adding the numbers.

■ Include pictures at each station to show students proper form for the skill or activity they are to do.

■ For the student who is overweight/obese, design the station activities to allow for various levels or ways the student could complete the activity, thus assuring a level of success. Introduce this student to an initial activity or arrange the starting place of stations from easiest to most difficult.

ASSESSMENT

■ Distribute one copy of the Estimated Energy Expenditure for Common Activities Chart to each student. Go through an example as a class, then ask students to estimate the number of calories they used in today's activities. Discuss the results. Insights might include that students burned different amounts of calories and that different activities expend different amounts of calories, just as different foods contain different amount of calories.

■ When revisiting the activity, circulate among stations, asking questions to review the Estimated Energy Expenditure for Common Activities Chart and its relationship to students' activities.

■ Ask students these questions, either as a class, in small groups, or on a quiz:
  • What is energy balance?
  • How does the amount of physical activity you perform affect the amount of food you should eat?
  • How does physical activity impact growth and development?

6.6 Cross-Training Triumph

HIGH SCHOOL

Growth and development—A healthy body composition can be achieved and maintained in part through a combination of physical activity and moderate diet. Muscular strength and endurance training promotes the maintenance and growth of muscle, which expends more calories at rest than does fat. Aerobic fitness activities expend further calories.

PURPOSE

- Students will be able to explain the significance to body composition of combining strength training (promoting metabolically active lean tissue) and aerobic fitness (expending more calories).
- Students will design a fitness plan that includes both strength training and aerobic fitness training.

RELATIONSHIP TO NATIONAL STANDARDS

Physical Education Standard 4: Achieves and maintains a health-enhancing level of physical fitness.

Health Education Standard 1: Students will comprehend concepts related to health promotion and disease prevention.

EQUIPMENT

- 3 markers (one color per group)
- Jump ropes (several for Groups A and C)
- Aerobic step boxes (several for Group A)
- Basketballs (several for Groups A and C)
- Hand weights (several sets of varying weight for Groups B and C)
- Resistance tubing or elastic bands (several for Groups B and C)

PROCEDURE

1. Before class begins, place the required equipment in three distinctly separate areas of the activity space: the jump ropes, aerobic steps, and basketballs in one area for group A; the hand weights and resistance tubing in another area for group B; and more hand weights and basketballs in a third area for group C.

2. Post a Master Point Chart at the front of the room, and place three markers near the chart.

Reproducible

- Cross-Training Triumph Task Cards (make one copy of each of the three cards, one each for group A, B, and C)

Group A
Cross-Training Triumph Task Card

Every group member must perform each task before task name and points can be recorded on the master point chart.

Task 1: Jump rope 50 times = 70 points
Task 2: Jog three laps while dribbling a basketball = 50 points
Task 3: Do step aerobics: basic step for three minutes = 50 points
Task 4: Slide sideways around the perimeter of the activity area two times = 70 points

Activity 6.6 Cross-Training Triumph Task Card—Group A
From *Physical Best activity guide: Middle and high school levels*, 2nd edition, by NASPE, 2005, Champaign, IL: Human Kinetics.

Group B
Cross-Training Triumph Task Card

Every group member must perform each task before task name and points can be recorded on the master point chart.

Task 1: Shoulder press with hand weights (15 reps) = 70 points
Task 2: Lat raises with hand weights (15 reps) = 70 points
Task 3: Biceps curls (15 reps per arm) = 50 points
Task 4: Triceps extension with hand weights (15 reps per arm) = 50 points

Activity 6.6 Cross-Training Triumph Task Card—Group B
From *Physical Best activity guide: Middle and high school levels*, 2nd edition, by NASPE, 2005, Champaign, IL: Human Kinetics.

Group C
Cross-Training Triumph Task Card

Every group member must perform each task before task name and points can be recorded on the master point chart.

Task 1: Shoulder press with hand weights (15 reps) = 70 points
Task 2: Slide sideways around the perimeter of the activity area two times = 70 points
Task 3: Resistance tubing chest press (15 reps) = 70 points
Task 4: Jump rope 50 times = 70 points

Activity 6.6 Cross-Training Triumph Task Card—Group C
From *Physical Best activity guide: Middle and high school levels*, 2nd edition, by NASPE, 2005, Champaign, IL: Human Kinetics.

3. Divide students into three groups—A, B, and C—each of which will perform a different set of activities. Activities are listed on each group's Cross-Training Triumph Task Cards.

4. Read the following scenario to the class. Encourage students to think about the question during the lesson. Tell students that this question will be repeated and discussed at the conclusion of the lesson:

June is trying to lose weight and maintain her weight loss. She has been doing step aerobics three times a week, increasing her intensity each week. She lost weight for the first two months but then her progress stopped. What does June need to do differently with her workout?

5. Give each of the three groups a different Training Triumph Task Card. As a group finishes each task on their card, have them use their marker to record the name of the activity performed and the number of points earned on their section of the Master Point Chart.

6. Have groups continue this for each task listed on their card. Allow students 10 to 15 minutes to complete all of the tasks listed on their group's task card. Group C—who did the combined aerobic fitness and muscular strength and endurance training—will end up with the largest point total.

TEACHING HINTS

▦ If you do not have some of the equipment listed, substitute a different aerobic fitness activity or another muscular strength activity. Group A must have all aerobic activities, Group B must have all muscular strength activities, and Group C must have two of each. Be certain you change the task cards to reflect the substitutions. Possible substitutions include using stationary bicycles (aerobic fitness) and push-ups (muscular strength).

▦ Students who have experienced the activity in chapter 3 titled Cross-Training Trio may need you to clarify that there are many ways to define and apply cross-training principles. In the aerobic fitness activity, the focus was on crossing training among various muscle groups and joints while focusing solely on aerobic fitness development. In this activity, the focus is on crossing training among the various health-related fitness components to enhance body composition.

SAMPLE INCLUSION TIPS

General inclusion tip suggestions per each group activity:

- Aerobic step boxes: Allow student with disability to walk/run with partner or if student is using a wheelchair allow them to wheel for a designated time.
- Basketballs: Substitute smaller, lighter balls to complete activity.
- Basketball hoops: Substitute basketball hoops that can be lowered to ensure success. Pair the student with a disability with a peer buddy during activity to rebound balls in expedient fashion.
- Stationary bicycles: Great for most students with disabilities and particularly students with visual impairments, once on cycle, allow student with disability to have support of cycle through duration of activity. At completion of spinning on cycle, time or distance can be recorded.

Note: In general, recognize that with accommodations for strength, endurance, and power, for some students with disabilities, time may need to be decreased, rest periods may need to be increased, and in game situations, frequent rotation in and out of the game may be necessary.

ASSESSMENT

When all three groups have completed the activities listed on their task cards, ask the groups to gather around the Master Point Chart. Process the activity by asking the following:

- How many activities did each group complete? (4)
- Examine the large point chart and identify the difference in the tasks completed by each group. How do they differ? (Aerobic only, muscular only, and combination. The combination group received the most points.)
- What conclusion can you draw from this activity? (A combination of aerobic fitness and muscular strength and endurance conditioning has the greatest value to body composition by both expending calories through aerobic activity and promoting healthy lean body weight through muscle conditioning. This combination of activities has a positive effect on metabolism.)
- Re-present the situation read at the beginning of class:

  June is trying to lose weight and maintain her weight loss. She has been doing step aerobics three times a week, increasing her intensity each week. She lost weight for the first two months but then her progress stopped. What does June need to do differently with her workout? Using the information you gained in class today, design a new workout plan for June.

6.7

Health Quest

MIDDLE AND HIGH SCHOOL

Note: Students need to know compass basics before they participate in this activity.

Nutrition—There are six categories of nutrients: carbohydrates, proteins, fats, vitamins, minerals, and water. All of these are essential for good health. These nutrients are best obtained by eating a diet that contains a wide variety of foods from the groups listed on the Food Guide Pyramid, including grains, vegetables, fruits, dairy, proteins, and fats. In addition, students should drink 6 to 8 glasses of water a day, or more.

PURPOSE

Students will learn through discovery and discussion that eating a diet that provides all six categories of nutrients in sufficient amounts through a variety of foods will help them to achieve their "Physical Best."

RELATIONSHIP TO NATIONAL STANDARDS

Physical Education Standard 5: Exhibits responsible personal and social behavior that respects self and others in physical activity settings.

Health Education Standard 1: Students will comprehend concepts related to health promotion and disease prevention.

EQUIPMENT

- 7 to 10 compasses (one per group, with groups of two to four students at most)
- Flags, poly spots, hoops, or other objects that can serve as checkpoints

Reproducibles

- Checkpoint Signs, one sign per station (there are six stations)
- Health Quest Answer Sheets, one per student
- Food Guide Pyramid, one per student

Checkpoint One: Water

When health is absent,

(Write this phrase on line one on your Health Quest Answer Sheet, Part A.)

List five ways to get water into your diet and stay well hydrated on your Health Quest Answer Sheet, Part B, Checkpoint One.

Set your compass to this degree: _____

Go the following distance: _____

Activity 6.7   Checkpoint Signs
From *Physical Best activity guide: Middle and high school levels*, 2nd edition, by NASPE, 2005, Champaign, IL: Human Kinetics.

Name: _____ Class: _____ Date: _____

Activity 6.6
Health Quest Answer Sheet

Part A
Copy the line listed at each checkpoint.

Line one _____
Line two _____
Line three _____
Line four _____
Line five _____
Line six _____
Who is credited with this statement? _____
When is he believed to have written this? _____

Part B
List the five items requested at each checkpoint.

Checkpoint One: Water _____

Checkpoint Two: Carbohydrates _____

Checkpoint Three: Fats _____

Checkpoint Four: Proteins _____

Checkpoint Five: Vitamins _____

Checkpoint Six: Minerals _____

Activity 6.7   Health Quest Answer Sheet
From *Physical Best activity guide: Middle and high school levels*, 2nd edition, by NASPE, 2005, Champaign, IL: Human Kinetics.

Food Guide Pyramid

Concentrated fats, oils, & refined sugars
Use sparingly

Milk, yogurt, & cheese group
2-3 servings

Meat, poultry, fish dry beans, eggs, & nuts group
2-3 servings

Vegetable group
3-5 servings

Fruit group
2-4 servings

Bread, cereal, rice & pasta group
6-11 servings

Liquids
8-12 glasses

Activity 6.7   Food Guide Pyramid
From *Physical best activity guide: Middle and high school levels*, 2nd edition, by NASPE, 2005, Champaign, IL: Human Kinetics.

■ Pencils, one per student

■ *Teaching Orienteering* (optional; available from www.humankinetics.com)

PROCEDURE

1. Set up an orienteering course that has six checkpoints with the six checkpoint signs. Each sign contains blanks where you need to fill in the compass degrees and distances specific to your orienteering course.

2. Set up six incorrect checkpoints, so that not all points on the course are correct, and students must follow the compass and distance directions to get to the correct points.

3. Discuss the six categories of nutrients with the class. Pass out a copy of the Food Guide Pyramid to each student. Tell them that today they are going to participate in an activity that will explore the categories of nutrients. Tell students that people throughout history have recognized the importance of good health, and today they'll follow an orienteering course to discover one early scientist and philosopher's belief about good health. In the process, they'll also recall what they know of the six categories of nutrients.

4. Divide the class into as many teams as there are compasses and review compass basics:

- Tell students to hold the compass level on the palm of a hand so that the needle can float in the fluid freely to give a correct reading.

- Make sure that students know how to turn the amortization ring to the correct reading (the degree that they want to head off in should be lined up with the direction of travel arrow, also known as the orienteering arrow). For example, to go east, you would need to turn the amortization ring so that 90 degrees was lined up with the direction of travel arrow.

- Tell the students that they have to make sure that the red part of the arrow is pointing north. (The red arrow should be placed in the north alignment arrow outline that is located in the base of the compass housing. This is important because all bearings represent degrees from the north. The teacher or students could come up with a slogan that would remind students that before they travel in the direction that the travel arrow is pointing, that they must have the red magnetic north arrow placed in the direction of travel arrow, also known as the orienteering arrow).

- When the red arrow is pointing north and the amortization ring has the correct reading students can head off following the directional arrow on the base unit of the compass.

- Distance is important and can make the difference between checking in at the right or wrong checkpoint. Remind your students that they need to follow the distance directions carefully to locate the correct checkpoint.

5. Each group starts the course in two-minute intervals or more as time allows. Team members must try to find the correct checkpoints, copy the line of the saying, and answer the question about nutrition at each point.

TEACHING HINTS

- Students need to be able to calculate the distance they are traveling, whether it be in steps or yardage.
- It is helpful to set up the course so that it leads all the teams back to the starting point.
- Finding some permanent checkpoints on your school grounds will make it easier to set up a course. (For example, you might use the corner of the school to the softball backstop to the field hockey goal to the corner of the blacktop to the baseball backstop to the basketball hoop and back to the corner of the school.)
- Setting up a duplicate course with some slightly different checkpoints will force your students to follow the directions carefully.
- The poem used for this activity is credited to Herophiles, a Greek scientist, philosopher, and physician, and he was believed to have written this around 300 B.C.

SAMPLE INCLUSION TIPS

- Pair students with visual impairments with a buddy to guide them through the course or place directions on a portable tape player, giving directions of which way to face and how many steps to walk. For students with cognitive/learning disabilities, place student in center of team members in order to actively engage the student with a disability and proceed with activity.
- If you have students with ambulatory difficulties (crutches, braces, wheelchairs), make sure the course follows a smooth, wide path. Consider creating a "short course" for these students.

ASSESSMENT

- Students should turn in their completed Health Quest Answer Sheets to you for review.
- Ask the class: What are the categories of nutrients? What were some of their answers for each checkpoint?
- Ask students to log everything they eat for two days and categorize the foods and number of servings according to the Food Guide Pyramid.

6.8

Fast Food Frenzy

MIDDLE AND HIGH SCHOOL

Note: This activity requires that students have had several previous experiences using resistance bands, because they will be creating their own routines. See chapter 4 for resistance band activities.

Nutrition—Food habits developed in adolescence are the ones most likely to carry into adult life. Adolescents make many choices for themselves about what they eat. Social or peer pressures may push them to make both good and bad choices. Students acquire information, and sometimes misinformation, about nutrition from personal, immediate experiences. They are concerned with how food choices can improve their lives and looks now, so they may engage in crash dieting or the latest fad in weight gain or loss. Conversely, it is also common to see increased calorie consumption, especially of fats and carbohydrates, among adolescents.

PURPOSE

- Students will be able to select the healthiest sandwiches and salads available at given fast food restaurants.
- Students will name more healthful alternatives to high-calorie or high-fat foods.
- Students will design a nutrition health behavior contract.

RELATIONSHIP TO NATIONAL STANDARDS

Physical Education Standard 4: Achieves and maintains a health-enhancing level of physical fitness.

Physical Education Standard 5: Exhibits responsible personal and social behavior that respects self and others in physical activity settings.

Health Education Standard 1: Students will comprehend concepts related to health promotion and disease prevention.

Health Education Standard 6: Students will demonstrate the ability to advocate for personal, family, and community health.

EQUIPMENT

This is a comprehensive station activity that spans a two-day period. You may set up all of the stations or you may incorporate a few of these nutrition stations into your circuit training activities.

- "Ghostbusters" song and music player (*Ghostbusters: Original Soundtrack Album*; Various Artists; 1984, Elmer Bernstein. Release date: October 25, 1990. Label: Arista.)
- Resistance bands, one per student
- Bell, train whistle, or bicycle horn (to serve as the "fat buster signal")
- Large sheets of chart paper, one per group (same as number of stations)
- Wide-tip markers, one per group (same as number of stations)
- Masking tape
- Pencils, one per student

All other materials are listed by station:

- Station 1
  - 60 individually wrapped straws
  - 60 pieces of notebook paper
  - Cone
  - 60 pieces of construction paper
  - Trash can
  - Station 1 Instruction Poster: Unclog Those Arteries

- Station 2
  - 4 empty cans of different types of soda with the number of teaspoons of sugar that each contains written on bottom of each can
  - Measuring spoons: 1 teaspoon and 1 tablespoon
  - 4 cups (1 in front of each of the 4 sugary drinks)
  - Large bowl
  - 2 pounds of sand (to represent sugar)
  - Numbers to label each can or container (1, 2, 3, 4)
  - Station 2 Instruction Poster: Sugar Time

- Station 3
  - 7 yellow index cards. Each card lists 1 of the following food items: 1 chocolate brownie; 1 piece of devil's food cake; 1 cup ice cream; 1 cup soda pop; 1 ounce macadamia nuts; 12 potato chips; 1 teaspoon mayonnaise.
  - 7 pink index cards. Each card lists 1 of the following food items: 1 apple, 1 piece of angel food cake, 1 cup grape juice; 1 ounce almonds; 1 cup pretzels; 1 teaspoon yellow mustard.
  - Station 3 Instruction Poster: Instead of . . . Why Not Try
  - 4 copies of Calorie Charts, in folders

- Station 4
  - 60 Lunch Menu Suggestion Cards
  - 4 school lunch menus (listing five days of lunch menus for your school)
  - Station 4 Instruction Poster: Lunch Menu Suggestions
  - Suggestion box (shoe box, marked "Suggestion Card Deposit Box")

- Station 5
  - 5 small empty bags of snacks with nutritional information (corn chips, potato chips, mini cookies, pretzels, popcorn, and so on)
  - Station 5 Instruction Poster: Snack Attack
  - Pencils

- Station 6
  - Poster listing five different fast food sandwiches (could use empty sandwich containers or pictures of each sandwich to illustrate)
  - Copy of the nutritional information for each of the five sandwiches (find the nutritional information for each of the sandwiches by logging on to specific fast food restaurants' Web sites, such as www.mcdonalds.com; www.burgerking.com; www.hardees.com; www.pizzahut.com; www.tacobell.com)

- Folder labeled "Nutritional Info for Sandwich Choices"
- Station 6 Instruction Poster: Healthy Meal Deal: Sandwich

▨ Station 7

- Poster listing five different fast food restaurants' salads (could use pictures of each salad to illustrate)
- Copy of nutritional information for each of the salads (find nutritional information for each salad by logging on to the specific fast food restaurants' Web sites—don't forget salad dressing nutrition information)
- Folder labeled "Nutritional Info for Salad Choices"
- Station 7 Instruction Poster: Healthy Meal Deal: Salads

PROCEDURE

1. Before class, set up all nutrition stations around the perimeter of the activity area. Place the resistance bands randomly throughout the middle of the activity area.

Reproducibles

▨ Fast Food Frenzy Discovery Worksheet, one per student

▨ Calorie Chart

▨ Instructions for Stations, one at each station

▨ Lunch Menu Suggestion Card, two per student

▨ Health Behavior Contract, one per student

Activity 6.8
Fast Food Frenzy Discovery Worksheet

Station 1: Unclog Those Arteries

1. What did the two different pieces of paper represent?

2. What did pinching the straw represent?

3. What can clog up a person's arteries?

4. What was the purpose of this activity?

Activity 6.8 Fast Food Frenzy Discovery Worksheet
From Physical Best activity guide: Middle and high school levels, 2nd edition, by NASPE, 2005, Champaign, IL: Human Kinetics.

Calorie Chart

Food Item	Serving	Calories per serving
Almonds	1 ounce	165
Apple	1	80
Angel food cake	1 piece	125
Brownie	1 piece	100
Devil's food cake	1 piece	235
Fruit juice	1 cup	115
Ice cream	1 cup	115
Macadamia nuts	1 ounce	22
Mayonnaise	1 tablespoon	100
Mustard (yellow)	1 teaspoon	5
Potato chips	10	105
Pretzels	10	240
Soda	1 can	150
Yogurt, frozen (low-fat)	1 cup	230

www.caloriechart.org

Activity 6.8 Calorie Chart
From Physical Best activity guide: Middle and high school levels, 2nd edition, by NASPE, 2005, Champaign, IL: Human Kinetics.

Station 1
Unclog Those Arteries

1. Each person takes one straw.
2. Using the straw, try to pull up and hold a piece of notebook paper while you walk around the cone (that is six feet away) and back to the station. Lay the notebook paper back in its original spot.
3. Using the straw, try to pull up and hold a piece of colored construction paper while walking around the cone and back to the station. Lay the construction paper back in its original spot.
4. Now, pinch the straw in the middle and once again try to pull up and hold the notebook paper, and then the construction paper.
5. Place your straw in the trashcan.
6. Using the title of this station as a hint, answer the station 1 questions on your Fast Food Frenzy Discovery Worksheet.

Activity 6.8 Instructions for Stations
From Physical Best activity guide: Middle and high school levels, 2nd edition, by NASPE, 2005, Champaign, IL: Human Kinetics.

Lunch Menu Suggestion

I think we should eliminate _____

from our menu at school because it is not a healthy food choice.

Instead, I think we should add _____
to the menu because it would be a healthier alternative.

Thank you.
Sincerely,

Activity 6.8 Lunch Menu Suggestion Cards
From Physical Best activity guide: Middle and high school levels, 2nd edition, by NASPE, 2005, Champaign, IL: Human Kinetics.

✂ - - - - - - - - - - - - - - -

Lunch Menu Suggestion

I think we should eliminate _____

from our menu at school because it is not a healthy food choice.

Instead, I think we should add _____
to the menu because it would be a healthier alternative.

Thank you.
Sincerely,

Activity 6.8 Lunch Menu Suggestion Cards
From Physical Best activity guide: Middle and high school levels, 2nd edition, by NASPE, 2005, Champaign, IL: Human Kinetics.

✂ - - - - - - - - - - - - - - -

Lunch Menu Suggestion

I think we should eliminate _____

from our menu at school because it is not a healthy food choice.

Instead, I think we should add _____
to the menu because it would be a healthier alternative.

Thank you.
Sincerely,

Activity 6.8 Lunch Menu Suggestion Cards
From Physical Best activity guide: Middle and high school levels, 2nd edition, by NASPE, 2005, Champaign, IL: Human Kinetics.

Activity 6.8
Health Behavior Contract

Write out your contract, filling in numbers 1-4. After every seven days, evaluate how your diet change plan is working. You can add this contract to your physical education journal or portfolio.

1. One healthful change I want to make is:

2. How will this change positively affect my health:

3. My multi-step action plan for making this change is:

4. My chart to track my daily progress toward achieving this diet change:

Activity 6.8 Health Behavior Contract
From Physical Best activity guide: Middle and high school levels, 2nd edition, by NASPE, 2005, Champaign, IL: Human Kinetics.

2. At the beginning of the activity, ask the following questions:

   • What is fast food?

   • How can eating fast food frequently impact a person's diet?

   • Why do people choose to eat fast foods?

   • What are some fast foods that may actually be nutritious?

© Human Kinetics

3. Explain that this activity will help students discover some interesting facts about fast foods and snacks.

4. Briefly outline the purpose of each station.

5. Distribute a Fast Food Frenzy Discovery Worksheet to each student.

6. Divide students into seven groups (or the number of stations you have) and assign each group to a station. Emphasize the importance of students following the directions posted at each station and staying on task.

7. Explain that when the "fat buster signal" sounds they move to the next station.

8. Tell students that when the *Ghostbusters* song plays, they need to move to the center area, select a resistance band, and choose their own resistance band exercise until the music stops. Instruct them to leave their worksheet and pencil neatly at the station before coming to the center. Play the music after students complete every second (every other) station, not after each station.

9. If students can handle this appropriately, ask them to substitute the words "Fat Busters" for the word "Ghostbusters" in the song. In other words, when the song says "Ghostbusters," the students shout "Fat Busters" instead.

10. When the music stops, have students carefully lay down their resistance bands, pick up their pencils and sheets, and move to the next nutrition station.

11. At the end of the station activity, give each group a large sheet of paper and a marker. Ask students to use the chart paper to answer the following questions in their group.

    • What was the most shocking fact you learned at the nutrition stations?

    • What specific diet change do you recommend that teens make to maintain a healthy diet?

    • What other areas of nutrition would you like to explore?

    • What questions do you have about the nutrition stations?

12. Ask each group to post their chart paper around the room.

TEACHING HINTS

■ Use alternate physical activities instead of resistance band exercises in the center area.

■ If using the first assessment idea, before this lesson, teach students the process for developing a health behavior contract.

■ Have students design additional nutrition stations that could be used at a later date.

■ Use only one or two stations at a time as part of an activity circuit (e.g., muscular strength and endurance), until you've covered all seven stations with all students.

■ At first glance, this activity may seem like a lot of work to prepare. Use these tips to minimize your preparation time:

• Well ahead of time, ask students to gather and prepare as many of the materials needed as possible, one or a pair of students per station. Simply review and refine their work before using it in class. Reimburse for small items, such as straws, if receipts are presented. If appropriate, offer extra credit for this help.

• Cut your future preparation time for revisiting this activity: Laminate cards and posters, then place each station's small items in a zip-type bag, clip large items to the bag, and place all seven stations' materials in a large bin. Simply pull out the bin when you repeat the activity.

■ For safety's sake, remind students to stay in their own space when using resistance bands.

■ To reduce time spent writing, have groups designate a "recorder" to complete one worksheet per group, and have a spokesperson present the answers for one station from the worksheet instead of creating a large chart.

SAMPLE INCLUSION TIPS

■ Use the designated "recorder" teaching tip to assist those students who have difficulty transferring their thoughts to written word.

■ For students with only upper body capabilities, encourage student to use bands to further develop upper body strength.

ASSESSMENT

■ Ask students individually or as a group to fill out a Health Behavior Contract.

■ Have each group choose a spokesperson to present their contract to the entire class. (See step 11 under "Procedure.")

6.9 Mass Metabolism

MIDDLE SCHOOL

Metabolism includes all the reactions the body uses to obtain and spend energy. Your body's top priority in life is to fuel the cells to keep them alive. When you don't eat, the body must turn to other sources for fuel. This may be the energy reserves of carbohydrates and fats in the cells or the proteins in your muscles. When you eat too much over a period of time, the unused energy will be deposited into a "savings account" (usually fat) to be withdrawn later for energy.

Nutrition—There are six categories of nutrients: carbohydrates, proteins, fats, vitamins, minerals, and water. All of these are essential for good health. These nutrients are best obtained by eating a diet that contains a wide variety of foods from the groups listed on the Food Guide Pyramid, including grains, vegetables, fruits, dairy, proteins, and fats. Fiber, found in food such as whole grains, can help to remove fats (cholesterol) from the blood. In addition, students should drink six to eight glasses of water a day, or more.

PURPOSE

Students will understand the following:

- Both physical activity and a balanced diet are essential to health-related fitness.
- Expending fats releases heat (energy) and calories. Consuming fiber helps to remove fats (cholesterol) from the blood.
- The body's metabolism is regulated by energy needs. Energy from nutrients supports every activity from mild to vigorous intensity.

RELATIONSHIP TO NATIONAL STANDARDS

Physical Education Standard 3: Participates regularly in physical activity.

Physical Education Standard 4: Achieves and maintains a health-enhancing level of physical fitness.

Health Education Standard 3: Students will demonstrate the ability to practice health-enhancing behaviors and reduce health risks.

EQUIPMENT

- 30 fleece (or yarn) balls (all the same color), to represent fat deposits
- 50 balls (varied size, color, texture), to represent other nutrients (carbohydrates, protein, vitamins, minerals, water), fiber, and metabolism
- 2 goals (e.g., hula hoops, indoor soccer goals, or trash cans)

Reproducible

- Metabolism Log, one per student (optional)

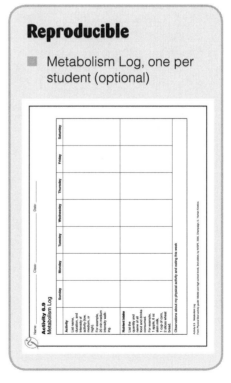

■ 2 yellow scrimmage vests, to represent fiber nutrients

■ Red scrimmage vests for team 1

■ Blue scrimmage vests for team 2

PROCEDURE

1. Define the terms used in the activity: nutrients (fats, carbohydrates, protein, vitamins, minerals, water), fiber, and metabolism. Explain their relationship to physical activity and their role in overall body composition.

2. Divide the class into two teams. Each team starts with three fat deposits (fleece balls) in their goal.

3. Designate one person from each team as fiber:

- The student playing fiber wears a yellow scrimmage vest.

- The student playing fiber is allowed to remove one fat deposit at a time from his or her own goal.

- The student playing fiber may not remove another fat deposit from his or her own goal until the first fat deposit is put into the opponent's goal.

4. Players may spread throughout the entire playing area. The game begins with all players stationary except for the fiber from each team. (Fibers are allowed to move.) The object of the game is to pass the fat deposit to teammates in order to put it into the opponent's goal.

5. Once one fat deposit has been removed, the instructor rolls out one nutrient ball into the playing area. Any player may pick up a nutrient ball as long as the player's feet are stationary. Players then pass the nutrient ball until it is dropped into the team's own goal. Teams try to get as many nutrient balls as they can into their own goals. Once the nutrient ball is in a goal it cannot be removed. The instructor adds nutrient balls one at a time into the playing area at a pace of the teacher's choosing throughout the entire game.

6. After a short period of play, the game is paused for the following changes:
- A new student is chosen to play the role of fiber.
- Select two students from each team. Allow these students to be able to move throughout the playing area, increasing the metabolic rate. These students play offense only—they can run with the ball, help pass the ball, retrieve balls, remove fat deposits, and place nutrient balls in the goals.
- Add three more fat deposits to each team's goal.
- Take a moment to reflect on how the game is progressing (e.g., the pace of the game, removal of fat deposits, or retrieving of nutrient balls).

7. Restart the game.

8. At three-minute intervals, stop the game to do the following:
- Select new fibers.
- Increase the number of moving players by two.
- Add three fat deposits to each goal.
- Continue to add nutrients throughout the game.
- Continue to reflect on how the game is progressing.

9. After the game is over, hand out the task sheets to students. Give them 10 to 15 minutes to complete the task sheets.

TEACHING HINT

As an extension, have students keep a weekly log to record physical activity, food intake, and observations on their week (see Metabolism Log on the CD-ROM).

SAMPLE INCLUSION TIPS

- For students with cognitive/learning disabilities and a variety of other disabilities, use peer buddy to assist with staying on task and to model appropriate movement of activity.
- Provide visual aids/pictures as necessary for understanding vocabulary.
- Utilize verbal prompting to repeat directions and check for understanding.

ASSESSMENT

- Ask students these questions:
  - What was the activity intensity like in the beginning of the game compared to the end of the game?
  - What was the role of fiber in the game? How does fiber relate to nutrition and body composition?
  - How do different nutrients, activity level, and the expending off of fat affect metabolism?
- Collect the Metabolism Log from each student and lead a class discussion on them. Check their written observations for understanding of the concepts.

Combined-Component Training

Chapter Contents

- Teaching Guidelines for Combined-Component Training
- Motor Skill Development Through Combined-Component Training
- Activities

© Human Kinetics

The concepts presented in this chapter provide adolescents the opportunity to engage in activities that combine multiple components of health-related fitness. In addition, activities can be adapted up or down so that at the middle school level, students engage in activities that reinforce the principles and guidelines introduced at the elementary level. At the high school level, students apply their knowledge in a way that involves decision making, goal setting, and individual choice.

Teaching Guidelines for Combined-Component Training

The activities in this chapter are designed to teach and reinforce the following concepts:

- Definition and identification of health-related and skill-related fitness components
- Benefits of health-related fitness
- Exploring options and making choices in health-related fitness activities

To maximize the benefits from these activities, students should have a basic knowledge of the individual components of fitness. If they have not been exposed to these principles, the previous chapters will be useful in helping you teach those concepts. For students already familiar with fitness concepts and activities, the previous chapters will allow for reinforcement of that information and behavior. In carrying out these activities, you are encouraged to provide individual choices so that students may challenge themselves at their level and participate in activities that are appropriate for their interests and goals.

Motor Skill Development Through Combined-Component Training

You can easily infuse motor skill and sport skill development into many of the activities of the unit you are teaching, allowing you to extend the length of the activity and provide variety. Many of the teaching hints contain ideas for carrying out sport-specific variations. This will allow students to connect fitness to other physical activities.

Activities

Chapter 7 Activities Grid

Activity number	Activity title	Activity page	Concept	Middle school	High school	Reproducible (on CD-ROM)
7.1	Match the Components	140	Definition	•	•	Health-Related Fitness Activity Cards
7.2	Health-Related, Skill-Related Circuit	142	Definition	•	•	Fitness Components Circuit Instructions
						Fitness Components Identification Circuit Worksheet
						Fitness Components Identification Circuit Posters
						Fitness Components Identification Circuit Answer Key
7.3	Health and Fitness Treasure Hunt	145	Health benefits	•	•	Health and Fitness Treasure Hunt Task Cards
7.4	Fortune Cookie Fitness	147	Exploring options and making choices	•	•	Fitness Fortunes
7.5	Circuit Training Choices	150	Exploring options and making choices	•	•	Circuit Training Choices Signs
7.6	Fitness Unscramble	152	Exploring options and making choices	•	•	Fitness Unscramble Task Cards
						Fitness Unscramble Worksheet
						Fitness Unscramble Worksheet Answer Key
7.7	Jump Bands Fitness	154	Exploring options and making choices	•	•	None
7.8	Partner Racetrack Fitness	157	Exploring options and making choices	•	•	Racetrack Signs
7.9	12 Ways to Fitness	159	Exploring options and making choices	•	•	Add-On Cards
7.10	Sporting Fitness	162	Exploring options and making choices	•	•	Sporting Fitness Activity Charts
						Sporting Fitness Soccer Drills

7.1 Match the Components

MIDDLE AND HIGH SCHOOL

Aerobic fitness is the ability to perform large muscle, dynamic, moderate to high intensity exercise for prolonged periods (ACSM 2000, p. 68). **Muscular strength** is the ability of a muscle or muscle group to exert a maximal force against a resistance one time through the full range of motion. **Muscular endurance** is the ability of a muscle or muscle group to exert a submaximal force repeatedly over a period of time. **Flexibility** is the ability to move a joint through its complete range of motion (ACSM 2000). **Body composition** is the amount of lean body mass (all tissues other than fat, such as bone, muscle, organs, and body fluids) compared to the amount of body fat, usually expressed in terms of percent body fat.

PURPOSE

- Students will review the five health-related fitness components.
- Students will be able to match the health-related fitness components (aerobic fitness, muscular strength and endurance, and flexibility) with a corresponding activity that illustrates that component.

RELATIONSHIP TO NATIONAL STANDARDS

Physical Education Standard 4: Achieves and maintains a health-enhancing level of physical fitness.

Physical Education Standard 5: Exhibits responsible personal and social behavior that respects self and others in physical activity settings.

EQUIPMENT

- Equipment as needed for students to complete their warm-ups as determined by the cards used
- Fast-paced music and music player

PROCEDURES

1. Briefly review the five health-related fitness components (aerobic fitness, muscular strength, muscular endurance, flexibility, and body composition).

2. Distribute one Health-Related Fitness Activity Card to each student. Use those provided on the CD-ROM or adapt the activities to fit your class's interests and available equipment.

3. Ask students to form groups of three; each person in the group must have a card that illustrates one of the following health-related fitness components. One

Reproducible

- Health-Related Fitness Activity Cards, one per student

Basketball

Activity 7.1   Health-Related Fitness Activity Cards
From *Physical Best activity guide: Middle and high school levels*, 2nd edition, by NASPE, 2005, Champaign, IL: Human Kinetics

Jump Rope

Activity 7.1   Health-Related Fitness Activity Cards
From *Physical Best activity guide: Middle and high school levels*, 2nd edition, by NASPE, 2005, Champaign, IL: Human Kinetics

Line Dance

Activity 7.1   Health-Related Fitness Activity Cards
From *Physical Best activity guide: Middle and high school levels*, 2nd edition, by NASPE, 2005, Champaign, IL: Human Kinetics

Step Aerobics

Activity 7.1   Health-Related Fitness Activity Cards
From *Physical Best activity guide: Middle and high school levels*, 2nd edition, by NASPE, 2005, Champaign, IL: Human Kinetics

Jog

Activity 7.1   Health-Related Fitness Activity Cards
From *Physical Best activity guide: Middle and high school levels*, 2nd edition, by NASPE, 2005, Champaign, IL: Human Kinetics

person should have a card that illustrates an aerobic fitness activity, one should have a card that illustrates a muscular strength or muscular endurance activity, and one a flexibility activity.

4. When the group is ready, the teacher checks the group's cards for accuracy. Once a group has these components represented, ask the group to create a warm-up that includes aerobic fitness, muscular strength and endurance, and flexibility.

5. The individual groups then perform their warm-up to music in preparation for the day's activity.

© Human Kinetics

TEACHING HINTS

- Laminate the cards so that they can be used repeatedly.
- In subsequent lessons, select a group to lead the class in their warm-up.

SAMPLE INCLUSION TIP

For students with visual or reading disabilities, pair with a peer who can read and explain what is written on the card, so both may complete the activity.

ASSESSMENT

- At the end of the period, collect the Health-Related Fitness Activity Cards. Ask students to classify each card into the category of aerobic fitness, muscular strength/muscular endurance, or flexibility. Do this as a class or have students do this individually for cards you have selected, by writing answers on a sheet of paper for your review.
- Discuss which of the cards could have multiple classifications.

7.2   Health-Related, Skill-Related Circuit

MIDDLE AND HIGH SCHOOL

The **health-related fitness** components are aerobic fitness, flexibility, muscular strength, muscular endurance, and body composition. The **skill-related fitness** components are agility, balance, coordination, power, reaction time, and speed.

PURPOSE

Students will distinguish among and identify the five health-related and six skill-related components of fitness.

RELATIONSHIP TO NATIONAL STANDARDS

Physical Education Standard 1: Demonstrates competency in motor skills and movement patterns needed to perform a variety of physical activities.

Physical Education Standard 5: Exhibits responsible personal and social behavior that respects self and others in physical activity settings.

EQUIPMENT

Equipment is determined by the circuit stations used. If using all stations on the CD-ROM, equipment needed includes the following:

- Pencils
- Stopwatches
- Table
- Rulers
- Floor tape
- Exercise mats
- Coins
- Basketballs
- Yardsticks
- Chairs with armrest
- Three 3/4-inch wood dowels that are each three feet long
- Singles jump ropes
- Balance boards

PROCEDURE

1. Create a series of stations that will help students identify the five health-related and six skill-related components of fitness. Use those provided on the CD-ROM, or modify these stations as your activity area will allow, and place a poster at each station. Give each student a Circuit Instructions and Worksheet copied double-sided. If you do adjust the posters and worksheet to fit the number of stations, make sure to include at least one station for each of the five health-related components and one station for each of the six skill-related components.

Reproducibles

- Fitness Components Circuit Instructions
- Ftness Components Identification Circuit Worksheet, one per student
- Fitness Components Identification Circuit Posters, one for each station
- Fitness Components Identification Circuit Answer Key

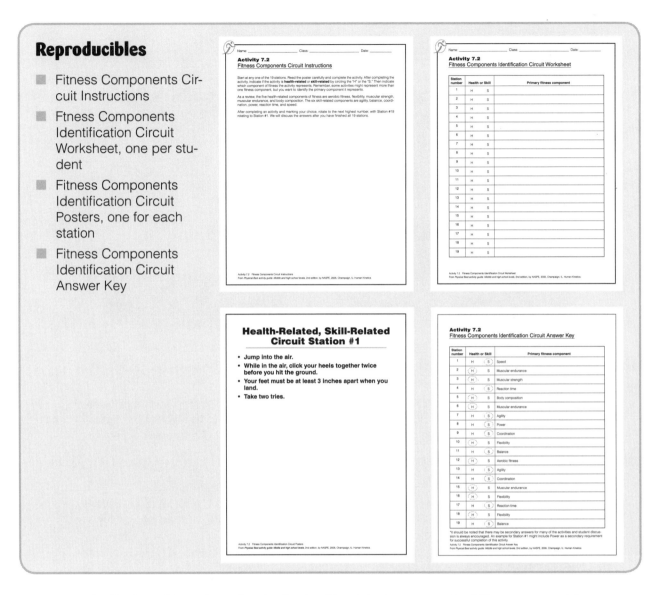

2. Review with students that the five health-related components of fitness are aerobic fitness, flexibility, muscular strength, muscular endurance, and body composition. The six skill-related components are agility, balance, coordination, power, reaction time, and speed.

3. Divide students into groups of two or three students per group. Have groups start at any one of the stations. Instruct them to read the poster at the station and complete the activity. After completing the activity, students should indicate if the activity is health-related or skill-related by circling the H or the S on their worksheets. Then students should indicate which specific (health-related or skill-related) component the activity represents.

4. After students complete an activity and mark their choices, on a signal from the teacher, the students rotate to the next highest numbered station, with students at the highest numbered station rotating to the lowest numbered station.

TEACHING HINTS

- Tell the students that some exercises may measure more than one component of fitness, but they should attempt to identify the most prominent skill.

- For more advanced students, do not provide the instructions page, so that they have to recall the fitness components from memory.
- Discuss the importance of both sets of components. For example, health-related fitness components focus on developing a health-enhancing level of physical fitness. Skill-related components focus on developing the skills to enjoy a variety of activities.

SAMPLE INCLUSION TIP

For students with physical disabilities, depending on the type and level of severity, student may participate in all or some of the activity components, or may be involved in identification process of the components.

ASSESSMENT

After all students have completed the stations in the circuit and recorded their answers, discuss the answers with them in a group setting. Have students justify why they have chosen a particular answer. Help students understand that both health- and skill-related components may be included in an activity.

7.3 Health and Fitness Treasure Hunt

MIDDLE AND HIGH SCHOOL

Health benefits—Regular participation in physical activity leads to many health benefits, including healthy body composition, increased self-confidence and self-esteem, greater energy, reduced stress and tension, and decreased risk of disease and obesity.

PURPOSE

To reinforce positive lifestyle choices and how they affect health and fitness.

RELATIONSHIP TO NATIONAL STANDARDS

Physical Education Standard 4: Achieves and maintains a health-enhancing level of physical fitness.

Physical Education Standard 6: Values physical activity for health, enjoyment, challenge, self-expression and/or social interaction.

Health Education Standard 1: Students will comprehend concepts related to health promotion and disease prevention.

EQUIPMENT

Task cards and equipment as determined by selected tasks. The sample task cards on the CD-ROM require these items:

- Several jump ropes
- Several tennis balls
- Exercise mats
- Basketballs and hoop

PROCEDURE

1. Develop a group of Treasure Hunt Task Cards listing specific risk behaviors and health-enhancing behaviors along with fitness and motor skill activities that help students understand the relationship between physical activity and a healthy lifestyle. See the samples on the CD-ROM.

2. Have students form groups of two or three. Place the task cards face down in the center of the activity area.

3. On the start signal, all students begin to jog around the perimeter of the activity area. On a signal, one person from each group runs to the center and takes a card, returns to the group, reads the card, and the group members perform the selected activity.

Reproducible

- Health and Fitness Treasure Hunt Task Cards

The use of tobacco products has been shown to cause cancer, heart disease, and lung disease. Aerobic fitness is also decreased when a person uses tobacco products.

Activity:

Jump rope 100 turns: Jump rope 50 turns, walk a lap, and then jump 50 turns again. The second 50, when you are already tired, represents the effects of tobacco products.

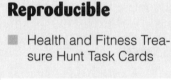

Activity 7.3 Health and Fitness Treasure Hunt Task Cards
From *Physical Best activity guide: Middle and high school levels*, 2nd edition, by NASPE, 2005, Champaign, IL: Human Kinetics.

4. When the activity is completed, the group begins to jog, and after completing one lap, another member of each group returns the card to the center, places it face down, and picks up another card.

5. Continue the activity for 5 to 10 minutes.

6. Use the first assessment as closure.

TEACHING HINTS

- Direct students not to read the card until they have returned to their group.

- If motor skills, such as the basketball spot-shot, are used, designate a specific area for those activities.

- Keep tasks simple and modify them for varying ability and developmental levels.

- Use higher-level concepts with grades 9 to 12.

SAMPLE INCLUSION TIP

For students with lower reading and/or ability levels, pair students with peers capable of reading and explaining information on card.

ASSESSMENT

- At the conclusion of the activity ask students to review what risk behaviors and health-enhancing behaviors they encountered. Ask for specific examples of both healthy and risky behaviors.

- Include some of the information learned in this activity on your next written test.

- If students use portfolios, have them list one or more health-enhancing or risk behaviors that were not used in the activity, and ask them to explain in their portfolio how exercise plays a role in each.

Modified from J. Carpenter and D. Tunnell, 1994. *Elementary P.E. Teacher's Survival Guide* (West Nyack, NY: Parker Publishing).

7.4 Fortune Cookie Fitness

MIDDLE AND HIGH SCHOOL

Exploring options and making choices—By experiencing a variety of fitness activities and then discussing them, students can gain an understanding of the importance of personal choices and preferences in maintaining lifetime physical activity.

PURPOSE

■ Students will explore and experience many types of exercise with different equipment while doing exciting and challenging physical fitness activities.

■ Students will learn fitness activities that are personally appealing.

■ Students will work cooperatively with partners.

RELATIONSHIP TO NATIONAL STANDARDS

Physical Education Standard 4: Achieves and maintains a health-enhancing level of physical fitness.

Physical Education Standard 5: Exhibits responsible personal and social behavior that respects self and others in physical activity settings.

Physical Education Standard 6: Values physical activity for health, enjoyment, challenge, self-expression and/or social interaction.

EQUIPMENT

■ Music and player

■ Equipment needed to complete the activities on the fortunes. If using fortunes provided on the CD-ROM, the following equipment is needed:

  • resistance bands
  • medicine balls

PROCEDURE

1. Write various fitness activities on strips of paper (Fitness Fortunes) with the time period or number of repetitions on the other side (Lucky Number). You can also use the Fitness Fortunes provided on the CD-ROM, which were made to fold so that the fitness fortune will appear on one side and the lucky number on the other. Place them in a "cookie jar" (or shoe box) in the center of the activity area. The activities can cover health-related fitness components as well as manipulative and nonlocomotor skills.

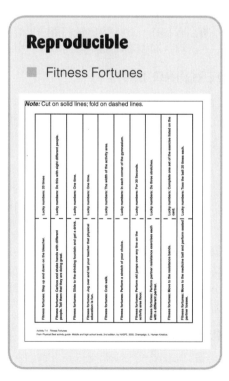

Reproducible

■ Fitness Fortunes

2. Explain to students that they'll select a fortune and then do the activity listed on the fortune for the time period or number of repetitions specified on the Lucky Number side.

3. Have students get into groups of two.

4. If using music, start the music.

5. Partners take turns selecting fitness fortunes from the box. The partners return to their buddy, and the two students complete the activity that is listed on the fortune for the amount of time or number of repetitions listed.

6. When both partners have completed the activity, the other partner comes to the box and exchanges the completed fortune for a new one.

TEACHING HINTS

■ On a particular day all of the fortunes can emphasize one of the health-related fitness components (e.g., aerobic fitness).

■ To incorporate progression and overload, encourage students to perform as many repetitions as possible while the music is playing and have them try to improve this number over time, when revisiting the activity.

■ If you do not include "Lucky Numbers" (the amount of time or number of repetitions) on your fortunes, you can instead use music taped to reflect 30 seconds of exercise and 10 seconds of silence to retrieve a new fortune.

SAMPLE INCLUSION TIP

For students with generally lower fitness levels, fortune cookies could contain two or more choices in the amount of activity (Lucky Numbers); this may enhance the concept of students "making choices."

ASSESSMENT

■ Have the students wear pedometers and record the number of steps that they take for the various fitness routines. Students can log their steps over a period of time and set some goals. These step counts can be graphed and used to compare activities and integrate math concepts with the routine.

■ Read aloud a question related to the purposes, and give partners a chance to discuss a correct response. Call on one pair to answer. Continue with several questions, soliciting answers from different pairs.

■ Ask students to write about how much they did or did not enjoy each of the Fitness Fortunes and why. They could write about how the routines affect health-related fitness and the importance of personal choice and preference in achieving and maintaining health-related fitness.

7.5 Circuit Training Choices

MIDDLE AND HIGH SCHOOL

Exploring options and making choices—By experiencing a variety of fitness activities and then discussing them, students can gain an understanding of the importance of personal choices and preferences in maintaining lifetime physical activity.

PURPOSE

- Students will explore and experience many types of exercise with different equipment while doing exciting and challenging physical fitness activities.
- Students will learn fitness activities that are personally appealing.
- Students will work cooperatively with partners or in small groups.

RELATIONSHIP TO NATIONAL STANDARDS

Physical Education Standard 3: Participates regularly in physical activity.

Physical Education Standard 4: Achieves and maintains a health-enhancing level of physical fitness.

Physical Education Standard 5: Exhibits responsible personal and social behavior that respects self and others in physical activity settings.

Health Education Standard 3: Students will demonstrate the ability to practice health-enhancing behaviors and reduce health risks.

EQUIPMENT

- Music and player
- Equipment needed to complete the activities on the Circuit Training Choices Signs. If using stations provided on the CD-ROM, equipment needed includes:
  - jump ropes
  - step benches (or stairs or bleachers)
  - resistance bands

PROCEDURE

1. Set up nine stations with three choices at each station. At each corner of the circuit is an aerobic fitness station (if using the Circuit Training Choices Signs on the CD-ROM, make two copies of each of the two "cardio-choice" stations). Another station is for abdominal strength. There are three flexibility stations: one for the legs, one for the torso area, and one for the upper body. An upper body strength station completes the circuit.

Reproducible

- Circuit Training Choices Signs

Cardio Choice

Jog
(around perimeter of area)

Jump Rope
(inside center of area)

Step-Ups
(use stairs, steps, or bleachers)

Activity 7.5 Circuit Training Choices Signs
From Physical Best activity guide: Middle and high school levels, 2nd edition, by NASPE, 2005, Champaign, IL: Human Kinetics.

2. Discuss with students the benefits of a circuit workout and of choice as it relates to fitness. (When you have a choice of exercises, you're more likely to find one that you like, and being able to do an activity that you like can help you be motivated to stay active.)

3. Have students get into equal groups and have each group select a station at which to start.

4. Students complete one of the activities listed at each station and move to the next station in a predetermined rotation pattern, on a signal or when they have completed their activity of choice.

© Human Kinetics

TEACHING HINTS

■ Program a music tape with multiple series of 30 seconds of music (work phase) with 10-second pauses (moving to next station). If available, you can also use a CD player and remote control for variable work and rest phases.

■ Remind students about choices and performing balanced workouts that include all of the components of health-related fitness.

SAMPLE INCLUSION TIP

For students who are overweight/obese, circuit training stations allow students to utilize time and adjust their personal intensity levels based on body type and current fitness level.

ASSESSMENT

■ Have students respond to the following questions after completing the circuit:
  • How is a circuit workout different than other workouts?
  • What factors influenced you to make the choices you did at each station?
  • What other choices might you add?
  • What can be the benefits of working with others when you exercise?

■ Have the students wear heart rate monitors and record their heart rates over the course of the circuit, and make observations regarding the various activities and stations.

■ Ask students to write about how much they did or did not enjoy each of the circuit activities and why. Have them explain how the circuit training affects health-related fitness. In addition, students could write their answers to the assessment questions rather than responding to the questions out loud.

■ If health-related fitness activities are done consistently throughout the year, students can measure their fitness levels using an appropriate fitness test (e.g., *FITNESSGRAM*). They can record their personal results in their journals and compare their results to previous tests. Students can then set new fitness goals for future testing.

7.6

Fitness Unscramble

MIDDLE AND HIGH SCHOOL

Exploring options and making choices—By experiencing a variety of fitness activities and then discussing them, students can gain an understanding of the importance of personal choices and preferences in maintaining lifetime physical activity.

PURPOSE

- Students will discriminate between health-related and skill-related components of fitness.
- Students will participate in group fitness and cooperative activities.

RELATIONSHIP TO NATIONAL STANDARDS

Physical Education Standard 1: Demonstrates competency in motor skills and movement patterns needed to perform a variety of physical activities.

Physical Education Standard 5: Exhibits responsible personal and social behavior that respects self and others in physical activity settings.

Health Education Standard 6: Students will demonstrate the ability to use goal-setting and decision-making skills to enhance health.

EQUIPMENT

- Foam ball
- 4-by-8-inch mat
- Volleyball or beach ball
- Long jump rope
- Rope ladder laid flat on the ground for agility course (alternatively, can use hula hoops)
- Blocks, five or six (as many as the highest number of students in a group)

Reproducibles

- Fitness Unscramble Task Cards, one per station
- Fitness Unscramble Worksheet, one per group
- Fitness Unscramble Worksheet Answer Key (for teachers only, not shown here)

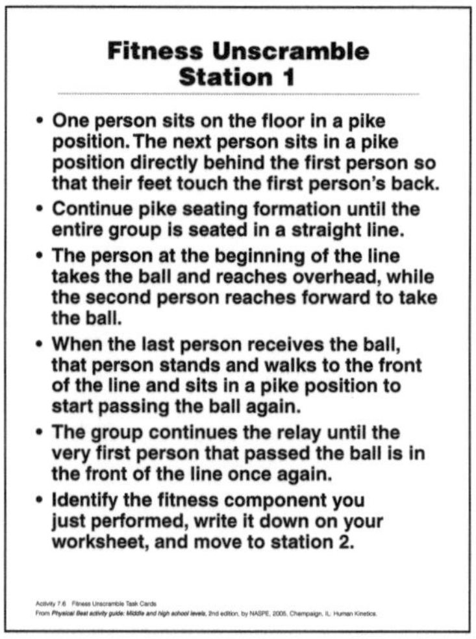

Fitness Unscramble
Station 1

- One person sits on the floor in a pike position. The next person sits in a pike position directly behind the first person so that their feet touch the first person's back.
- Continue pike seating formation until the entire group is seated in a straight line.
- The person at the beginning of the line takes the ball and reaches overhead, while the second person reaches forward to take the ball.
- When the last person receives the ball, that person stands and walks to the front of the line and sits in a pike position to start passing the ball again.
- The group continues the relay until the very first person that passed the ball is in the front of the line once again.
- Identify the fitness component you just performed, write it down on your worksheet, and move to station 2.

Activity 7.6 Fitness Unscramble Task Cards
From Physical Best activity guide: Middle and high school levels, 3rd edition, by NASPE, 2005, Champaign, IL: Human Kinetics.

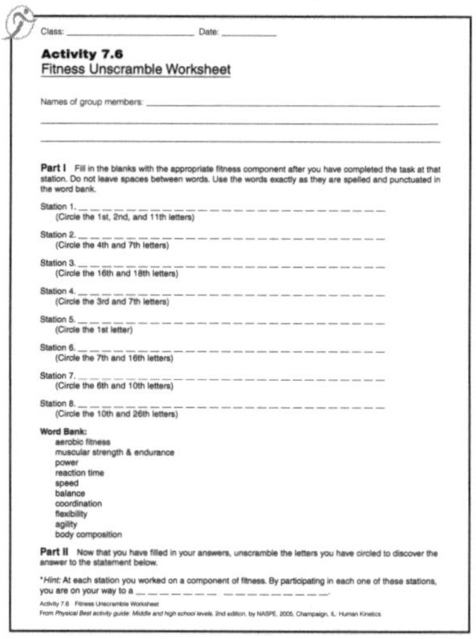

Class: _____ Date: _____

Activity 7.6
Fitness Unscramble Worksheet

Names of group members: _____

Part I Fill in the blanks with the appropriate fitness component after you have completed the task at that station. Do not leave spaces between words. Use the words exactly as they are spelled and punctuated in the word bank.

Station 1: _____
(Circle the 1st, 2nd, and 11th letters)
Station 2: _____
(Circle the 4th and 7th letters)
Station 3: _____
(Circle the 16th and 18th letters)
Station 4: _____
(Circle the 3rd and 7th letters)
Station 5: _____
(Circle the 1st letter)
Station 6: _____
(Circle the 7th and 16th letters)
Station 7: _____
(Circle the 8th and 10th letters)
Station 8: _____
(Circle the 10th and 26th letters)

Word Bank:
aerobic fitness
muscular strength & endurance
power
reaction time
speed
balance
coordination
flexibility
agility
body composition

Part II Now that you have filled in your answers, unscramble the letters you have circled to discover the answer to the statement below.

*Hint: At each station you worked on a component of fitness. By participating in each one of these stations, you are on your way to a _____

Activity 7.6 Fitness Unscramble Worksheet
From Physical Best activity guide: Middle and high school levels, 3rd edition, by NASPE, 2005, Champaign, IL: Human Kinetics.

- Poly spots, five or six (as many as the highest number of students in a group)
- Weighted backpack
- Medicine ball or weighted objects for backpack
- Exercise mats, enough for several students to use at once, connected together

PROCEDURE

1. Review the health-related and skill-related components of fitness as explained in Activity 7.2. Explain that the object of the activity is for groups of students to travel from station to station performing group fitness activities. After completing the tasks, groups determine the health-related or skill-related component used, and doing so gives them clues to complete the hint on the worksheet.

2. Divide class into small groups and send each group to a different station to begin.

3. Groups read the task card and perform the task given.

4. After completing the task, the group determines the health-related or skill-related fitness component used. Using the worksheet, students fill in the component with the corresponding station.

5. On a signal, groups rotate to the next numerical station. Once groups have rotated through each station, each group unscrambles the clues on the worksheet to solve the hint.

6. Reveal the answer to the hint. Assign each group a station and have them explain to the class why they chose the particular component they chose for that station.

TEACHING HINTS

- For an extension, as homework or a project, students can create an at-home fitness circuit that develops the skill-related or health-related components of fitness. They can design the circuit around their favorite sport or lifestyle physical activity.
- As a class, students can create their own circuit by having each group design a station.

SAMPLE INCLUSION TIP

For students using a wheelchair, allow student to decide level and type of participation in the variety of station activities. In order for students using a wheelchair to further develop upper body strength, student can be the rope turner or wheel/self-propel weaving through cones. For the volleyball station, allow student to catch ball or permit ball to bounce once before attempting to hit it back.

ASSESSMENT

- Have students discuss the differences between health-related and skill-related fitness. Do some stations seem to include more than one component?
- Observe cooperation among students during the station activities, and then ask the class what role group cooperation played in successful completion at stations.

7.7 Jump Bands Fitness

MIDDLE AND HIGH SCHOOL

Exploring options and making choices—By experiencing a variety of fitness activities and then discussing them, students can gain an understanding of the importance of personal choices and preferences in maintaining lifetime physical activity.

PURPOSE

- Students will explore and experience many types of exercise with different equipment while participating in exciting and challenging physical fitness activities.
- Students will work cooperatively in small groups.

RELATIONSHIP TO NATIONAL STANDARDS

Physical Education Standard 4: Achieves and maintains a health-enhancing level of physical fitness.

Physical Education Standard 5: Exhibits responsible personal and social behavior that respects self and others in physical activity settings.

EQUIPMENT

- A set of jump bands (2) for every three students
- Music and player

PROCEDURE

1. Divide the students into groups of three. Explain to students how to use the bands. Have two of the students in each group attach the jump bands around their upper ankles (they attach with Velcro). Have the third student step in and out of the bands as the students try to keep a 4/4 beat with the music. For the band holders, the movement is a constant repeated movement of "out," "out," "in," "in" (see diagram *a*).

2. Consider starting with music that has a clear beat, such as "We Will Rock You" or "Shrek #5." As the band holders begin jumping with their pattern, the middle jumper can begin with a simple "in," "in," "out" pattern with one foot. Then a two-foot pattern could be done the same way. Students switch from being a band holder to a middle jumper and back again as they get tired.

3. While jump band activities will develop muscular strength and endurance in lower body muscles, after several minutes of jumping, stop the entire class and have students perform a fun flexibility or upper body muscular strength and endurance activity to switch the fitness focus. During each break, give students two or three of these exercises to choose from, such as modified push-ups, floor/bench dips, or a stretch.

4. After the first break, put two groups together so that three students are holding the two sets of bands. One student has two sets of bands on his or her ankles. The remaining three students form a line and follow the leader through the two sets of bands (see diagram *b*).

Reproducible

- none

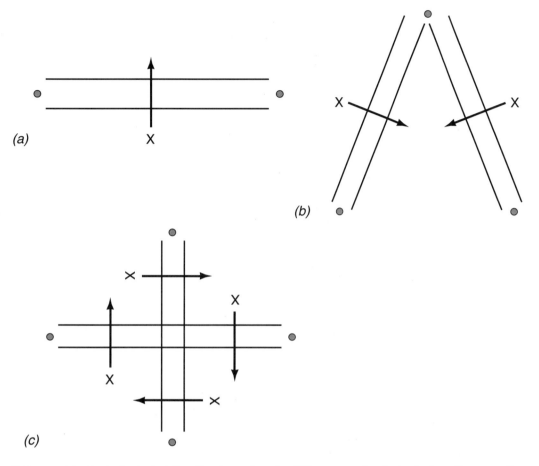

Dots represent students holding the jump bands. "X" represents students jumping over the bands.

5. After a few minutes, take another break to do additional flexibility and upper body muscular strength and endurance activities. Again, give students a variety of activities to choose from, such as calf stretches, hamstring stretches, push-ups, and sit-ups.

6. Finally, put the two groups together in a tic-tac-toe pattern and have the remaining two jumpers work their way around the pattern in front of the band holders. They could both go one direction and then change directions, or they could jump in opposite directions at the same time (see diagram *c*).

TEACHING HINTS

▨ Program a music tape with multiple series of 30 seconds of music with 10-second pauses. Have students switch roles during the pause and then start jumping when the music starts.

▨ Tell students that jumping is primarily an aerobic fitness activity. The activities they did during the breaks incorporated other components of health-related fitness.

▨ As a variation, try this:

• Use long jump ropes as your equipment.

• Place students in groups of three with a long jump rope for each group. The turners start turning the rope, and the jumpers come in and out of the rope with a "front-and-back-door" entrance. After each student has a chance to try each

position, have the jumper enter the rope, make three jumps, exit, go around one of the turners, and then come back in to the rope for three more jumps. Soon the jumping student will be making a figure eight around the turners, taking three jumps in the middle and continuing out to make the continuing figure eight. This should be done for 30 seconds, and then the students change positions and begin again. Jumping in this fashion is a demanding aerobic activity. Students get a rest while they are the turners of the rope.

SAMPLE INCLUSION TIP

Because there is a lot of jumping in this activity (for students with disabilities needing assistance with jumping and balance), consider using mini trampolines with braces/handles or provide a peer to extend a hand of support so student can simulate the jumping technique.

ASSESSMENT

■ Have the students wear pedometers and record the number of steps that they take during this activity. Ask students how many steps they took and if they are surprised by the number (which will likely be high). The step counts can be graphed and used to compare activities and integrate math concepts.

■ Have students describe how they could tell this was an aerobic fitness activity and explain how aerobic fitness affects health-related fitness. Ask students to comment on which of the "break," or "choice," activities align with each fitness component; separating those which are skill-related and health-related.

■ Lead a discussion related to the cooperation and team building necessary to experience success in this activity. What happened when they didn't listen to each other? How can cooperation and support be helpful in sticking with a physical activity plan?

Partner Racetrack Fitness

MIDDLE AND HIGH SCHOOL

Exploring options and making choices—By experiencing a variety of fitness activities and then discussing them, students can gain an understanding of the importance of personal choices and preferences in maintaining lifetime physical activity.

PURPOSE

- Students will explore and experience many types of exercise with different equipment while doing exciting and challenging physical fitness routines.
- Students will learn fitness activities that are personally appealing.
- Students will work cooperatively with partners.

RELATIONSHIP TO NATIONAL STANDARDS

Physical Education Standard 4: Achieves and maintains a health-enhancing level of physical fitness.

Physical Education Standard 5: Exhibits responsible personal and social behavior that respects self and others in physical activity settings.

Physical Education Standard 6: Values physical activity for health, enjoyment, challenge, self-expression and/or social interaction.

EQUIPMENT

- Music and player
- If using the signs provided on the CD-ROM, equipment needed includes:
  - resistance bands
  - free choice equipment—such as step benches and dumbbells

PROCEDURE

1. Arrange six stations in a circle or rectangle. At each station post a Racetrack Sign with several exercises or stretches to perform. Use those provided on the CD-ROM or design your own. If designing your own, include two aerobic, two muscular strength and endurance, and two flexibility stations.

2. Have students get into groups of two and select a station at which to begin. More than one pair might be at a station at one time.

3. On the start signal, one partner begins the first exercise or stretch at the sign while the other partner jogs around the perimeter of the stations.

Reproducible

- Racetrack Signs, a different sign for each station

Aerobic Fitness

- High knees
- Side shuffles
- Jumping jack variations
- Free choice-aerobic

4. Upon returning, the partners switch roles and pick a new exercise to perform. Repeat for each exercise.

5. After completing all of the activities at one station, students should run one lap and move to the next station.

TEACHING HINTS

- To add variety, change the locomotor skill for the students moving around the racetrack (e.g., jumping rope, sliding, carioca, or race walking).

- Let students design their own racetrack signs by creating a variety of manipulative activities (such as juggling, ball skills, or beanbag activities).

- This activity works well outdoors. Signs can be attached to slotted cones.

SAMPLE INCLUSION TIP

For students using a wheelchair, student can wheel/self-propel around racetrack while partner is exercising, recording time or distance traveled.

ASSESSMENT

- Students can use the Borg Rating of Perceived Exertion Scale to determine their level of intensity during this activity. This could be recorded on their activity logs. (The Borg Scale is included in Activity 3.9).

- If fitness activities are performed consistently throughout the year, students can measure their fitness levels using an appropriate fitness test (e.g., *FITNESSGRAM*). They can record their personal results in their journals and compare the results to previous tests. Students can then set new fitness goals to reach for future testing situations.

- After students have completed all activities, lead a discussion to encourage students to talk about what positive interactions emerged during the lesson. Did students get positive or negative feedback from their classmates, and how did this affect their motivation to continue participating?

- Have students record which activities they liked the least, which they liked the most, and how they could incorporate the activities they enjoyed into their physical activity plan.

7.9 12 Ways to Fitness

MIDDLE AND HIGH SCHOOL

Exploring options and making choices—By experiencing a variety of fitness activities and then discussing them, students can gain an understanding of the importance of personal choices and preferences in maintaining lifetime physical activity.

PURPOSE

- Students will explore and experience a variety of physical activities.
- Students will demonstrate and lead the class in activities.

RELATIONSHIP TO NATIONAL STANDARDS

Physical Education Standard 4: Achieves and maintains a health-enhancing level of physical fitness.

Physical Education Standard 5: Exhibits responsible personal and social behavior that respects self and others in physical activity settings.

Health Education Standard 3: Student will demonstrate the ability to practice health-enhancing behaviors and reduce health risks.

EQUIPMENT

Music and player

PROCEDURE

1. This is an add-on fitness game using 12 student leaders. Select the leaders and give each an Add-On Card.

2. The leaders will present the activity on their cards one at a time, with the class and leader performing repetitions of the exercise to match the leader number. For example, if Leader # 3 is presenting an exercise, that leader and the entire class will perform that exercise three times. Each new exercise is "added on" to the ones before it, with each exercise retaining its number of repetitions. The side box on page 160 shows a sample.

TEACHING HINTS

- Have student leaders select movements of their choice. You might have them select a movement from a sport or activity they enjoy.
- Select a dance that can be broken up into 12 parts (steps) to use as each add-on piece.

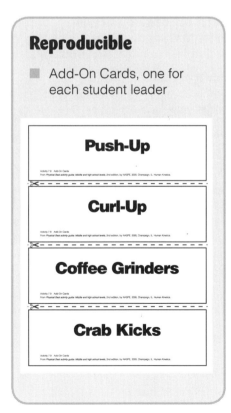

Reproducible

- Add-On Cards, one for each student leader

Push-Up

Activity 7.9   Add-On Cards
From *Physical Best activity guide: Middle and high school levels, 2nd edition*, by NASPE, 2005, Champaign, IL: Human Kinetics.

Curl-Up

Activity 7.9   Add-On Cards
From *Physical Best activity guide: Middle and high school levels, 2nd edition*, by NASPE, 2005, Champaign, IL: Human Kinetics.

Coffee Grinders

Activity 7.9   Add-On Cards
From *Physical Best activity guide: Middle and high school levels, 2nd edition*, by NASPE, 2005, Champaign, IL: Human Kinetics.

Crab Kicks

Activity 7.9   Add-On Cards
From *Physical Best activity guide: Middle and high school levels, 2nd edition*, by NASPE, 2005, Champaign, IL: Human Kinetics.

Sample Progression for Add-On Cards

Leader # 1: Push-Up
Leader and class do 1 push-up.

Leader # 2: Curl-Ups
Leader and class do 2 sit-ups and 1 push-up.

Leader # 3: Coffee Grinders
Leader and class do 3 coffee grinders, 2 sit-ups, and 1 push-up. In a coffee grinder the students are in a side leaning position, one hand on the floor with the same leg on floor—pivoting around the supporting hand.

Leader # 4: Crab Kicks
Leader and class do 4 crab kicks, 3 coffee grinders, 2 sit-ups, and 1 push-up. In a crab kick, students are in a crab walk position and lift one leg, hold, and switch legs.

Leader # 5: Golden Rests
Leader and class do 5 counts of golden rest, 4 crab kicks, 3 coffee grinders, 2 sit-ups, and 1 push-up. In a golden rest, the students simply rest for the number of counts desired.

Leader # 6: Leaping Leaps
Leader and class do 6 leaping leaps, 5 golden rests, 4 crab kicks, 3 coffee grinders, 2 sit-ups, and 1 push-up. In a leaping leap, students alternate right and left leading foot, leaping to the side.

Leader # 7: Jumping Jacks
Leader and class do 7 jumping jacks, 6 leaping leaps, 5 golden rests, 4 crab kicks, 3 coffee grinders, 2 sit-ups, and 1 push-up.

Leader # 8: Forward Lunges
Leader and class do 8 forward lunges, 7 jumping jacks, 6 leaping leaps, 5 golden rests, 4 crab kicks, 3 coffee grinders, 2 sit-ups, and 1 push-up.

Leader # 9: Carioca Steps
Leader and class do 9 carioca steps, 8 forward lunges, 7 jumping jacks, 6 leaping leaps, 5 golden rests, 4 crab kicks, 3 coffee grinders, 2 sit-ups, and 1 push-up.

Leader # 10: Skipping Skips
Leader and class do 10 skipping skips, 9 carioca steps, 8 forward lunges, 7 jumping jacks, 6 leaping leaps, 5 golden rests, 4 crab kicks, 3 coffee grinders, 2 sit-ups, and 1 push-up.

Leader # 11: Rooster Hops
Leader and class do 11 rooster hops, 10 skipping skips, 9 carioca steps, 8 forward lunges, 7 jumping jacks, 6 leaping leaps, 5 golden rests, 4 crab kicks, 3 coffee grinders, 2 sit-ups, and 1 push-up. In a rooster hop, students hop on one foot.

Leader # 12: Running Steps
Leader and class do 12 running steps, 11 rooster hops, 10 skipping skips, 9 carioca steps, 8 forward lunges, 7 jumping jacks, 6 leaping leaps, 5 golden rests, 4 crab kicks, 3 coffee grinders, 2 sit-ups, and 1 push-up. In running steps, the students jog in place.

© Human Kinetics

■ Use manipulative activities for each new add-on movement, such as juggling, ball skills, and beanbag activities.

SAMPLE INCLUSION TIP

For students with cognitive/learning disabilities, use pictures or a mnemonic memory device (abbreviation/acronym) to assist student in remembering what activity or skill is coming next.

ASSESSMENT

■ Ask students to write about how much they did or did not enjoy the add-on activity. How does each of the activities performed today contribute to health-related fitness? Which activities did they enjoy the most, and how might they incorporate those activities into their physical fitness plan?

■ Ask the class these questions: Which of the add-on activities did they enjoy the most? What other activities might students like to include the next time the class does this activity? How could you use the "add-on" concept in the fitness activities you do outside of class?

■ Observe and record physical and affective information. Which of the add-on activities do students need to improve in? Which students need direction in developing leadership skills?

Adapted, by permission, from P.E. Central, *Twelve Ways to Fitness*, www.pecentral.com/lesson ideas. Access date: 3/04.

7.10 Sporting Fitness

MIDDLE AND HIGH SCHOOL

Exploring options and making choices—By experiencing a variety of fitness activities and then discussing them, students can gain an understanding of the importance of personal choices and preferences in maintaining lifetime physical activity.

PURPOSE

Students will develop health-related fitness components as they practice sport skills. (This activity is written for soccer, but the same concept could be used in a variety of sports.)

RELATIONSHIP TO NATIONAL STANDARDS

Physical Education Standard 1: Demonstrates competency in motor skills and movement patterns needed to perform a variety of physical activities.

Physical Education Standard 4: Achieves and maintains a health-enhancing level of physical fitness.

EQUIPMENT

Equipment will vary based on the sport skills being taught. For the soccer activities presented in this activity, equipment needed includes:

- Soccer balls
- Cones (or lines)

PROCEDURE

1. Place the signs around the playing field, starting with a drill station and alternating with health-related fitness component stations. This will make 10 stations.

Reproducibles

- Sporting Fitness Activity Charts (five signs labeled with health-related fitness components and several options for exercises)
- Sporting Fitness Soccer Drills (five signs for soccer drills)

Flexibility

- Standing calf stretch
- Deep lunge right and left
- V-sit groin stretch

Activity 7.10 Sporting Fitness Activity Charts
From *Physical Best activity guide: Middle and high school levels*, 2nd edition, by NASPE, 2005, Champaign, IL: Human Kinetics.

Aerobic Fitness

- Agility ladder jumps
- Running cone obstacle course
- Bounding pattern

Activity 7.10 Sporting Fitness Activity Charts
From *Physical Best activity guide: Middle and high school levels*, 2nd edition, by NASPE, 2005, Champaign, IL: Human Kinetics.

Dribbling:

figure 8 format around cones

Activity 7.10 Sporting Fitness Soccer Drills
From *Physical Best activity guide: Middle and high school levels*, 2nd edition, by NASPE, 2005, Champaign, IL: Human Kinetics.

Passing:

to partner, 5-10 feet apart

Activity 7.10 Sporting Fitness Soccer Drills
From *Physical Best activity guide: Middle and high school levels*, 2nd edition, by NASPE, 2005, Champaign, IL: Human Kinetics.

2. Make sure students know what to do at each of the stations. Demonstrate how to do the sport-specific drills, and explain that students have a choice of exercises at the fitness component stations.

3. Divide students into 10 groups and place each group at one of the stations.

4. On your cue, have the students begin the activity labeled at their station.

5. After one to two minutes, cue the groups to switch stations in a clockwise fashion.

6. Once students have completed all stations, conduct a heart rate check. As time permits, continue through each station once more. After the second round, conduct another heart rate check.

TEACHING HINTS

■ Make your own skill-drill station signs for other sports and use this as a warm-up or conditioning activity for a variety of sports throughout the year.

■ Combine skills from various sports in the setup.

■ Increase the length of time at each station or the number of stations over time, when revising the activity.

SAMPLE INCLUSION TIPS

■ For students with low fitness levels, vary the activities on the station cards to build in success and serve as motivation to continue on to the next station. For example, use wall push-ups as a muscular strength and endurance activity option.

■ For students with high fitness levels, offer more challenging variations. For example, push-ups with feet slightly elevated, or with one ankle crossed over the other.

ASSESSMENT

■ Discuss with the students, or ask them for a written assessment as a homework assignment or in their journal, how skill-related and health-related fitness components affect soccer performance.

■ Discuss how students felt in the second round of stations compared with the first round. Did their aerobic and muscular endurance start to fade in the second round? What was their heart rate in the second round compared to the first? Did they feel more warmed up and flexible in the second round?

■ Ask students which activities they enjoyed the most and how they could incorporate those activities into their daily physical activity plans.

PART III

Personal Fitness Connections

CHAPTER

8

Self-Management and Goal Setting

© Human Kinetics

After your students learn about the benefits of physical activity and how much physical activity they need to get those benefits (see *Physical Education for Lifelong Fitness: The Physical Best Teacher's Guide, Second Edition*), the next important concepts to teach are how students can learn to become active if they are not already active and how they can stay active if they are currently active on a regular basis. To help you do this we have provided sample lesson plans, with support materials and suggested activities, for teaching self-management and goal setting.

These lessons are structured as a combination of lecture and activity. It is important to get across key concepts of self-management and goal setting, but we also want to provide an opportunity for students to be physically active. For both lessons, we first provide a lesson plan for the lecture portion of the class, along with support materials. Then we provide ideas that will help reinforce the lesson while providing an opportunity for the students to be physically active.

Activities

Chapter 8 Activities Grid

Activity number	Activity title	Activity page	Concept	Middle school	High school	Reproducible (on CD-ROM)
8.1	Learning Self-Management Skills	169	Self-management skills	●	●	What Stage Am I?
						Physical Activity Pyramid for Teens
	Enrichment Activity: Fitness Trail	172	Exercise	●	●	Fitness Trail Station Signs
8.2	Goal Setting	174	Goal setting	●	●	Setting Goals
						Short-Term Versus Long-Term Goals
	Enrichment Activity: School Stepping	175	Using a pedometer	●	●	School Stepping

8.1 Learning Self-Management Skills

MIDDLE AND HIGH SCHOOL

CONCEPT

Self-management skills—These skills are used by a person to take control of his or her lifestyle or behavior to stay physically active.

OBJECTIVES

- Describe the stages of physical activity change.
- Describe several different self-management skills.
- Explain how you can use self-management skills for living a healthy life.

OPENER

Introduce the lesson by using one of the following ideas:

- Show the class two contrasting photos—one of a person watching television, the other of a person being physically active in a small-group exercise. Have students provide ideas about why each person is behaving the way they are.
- In small groups, have students place famous people they know onto a physical activity spectrum (high amount of physical activity to low amount of physical activity).
- Place students in pairs and have them compare how each person manages and organizes the sports or physical activities they do. For example, do some students use a calendar to schedule their activity times? Do some students plan recreational activities for the days they don't have a sport practice session? (See table 8.1 for other self-management skills.)

Reproducibles

Use the following worksheet as homework or have students do it in class so that you can help them with questions.

- What Stage Am I?, one per student
- Physical Activity Pyramid for Teens, one per student (will be needed for class discussion)

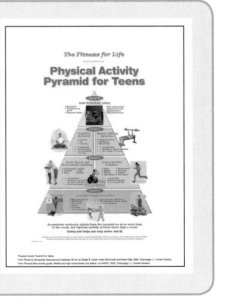

169

TABLE 8.1 Self-Management Skills for Active Living, Health, and Wellness

Skill	Definition
Self-assessment	This skill allows you to test your own fitness to help you see where you are and to help you get to where you want to be.
Building self-confidence	This skill helps you build the feeling that you are capable of being active for life.
Identifying risk factors	This skill helps you identify, assess, and reduce health risks.
Choosing good activities	This skill helps you select activities that are best for you personally.
Goal setting	This skill helps you set realistic and practical goals for being active and achieving physical fitness.
Building positive attitudes	This skill allows you to identify and build attitudes that will help you to be active throughout life.
Self-monitoring	This skill helps you learn to keep records (or logs) to see whether you are in fact doing what you think you are doing.
Finding social support	This skill helps you find ways to get the help and support of others (your friends and family) to adopt healthy behaviors and to stick with them.
Building performance skills	These skills help you to be good at and enjoy sports and other physical activities.
Building intrinsic motivation	This skill helps you learn to enjoy physical activity for your own personal reasons rather than because others think it is good for you.
Preventing relapse	This skill helps you stick with healthy behaviors even when you have problems getting motivated.
Managing time effectively	This skill helps you learn to schedule time efficiently so that you will have more time for important things in your life.
Building positive self-perceptions	This skill helps you think positively about yourself so you can stay active for a lifetime.
Learning to say "No"	This skill helps keep you from doing things you don't want to do, especially when you are under pressure from friends or other people.
Thinking critically	This skill helps you find and interpret information that will be useful in making decisions and solving problems.
Overcoming barriers	This skill helps you find ways to stay active despite barriers such as lack of time, unsafe places to be active, and weather.
Finding success	This skill helps you find success in physical activity.
Overcoming competitive stress	This skill helps you prevent or cope with the stresses of competition or the tension you feel when performing some types of activity.

TARGET QUESTIONS

1. What is the difference between a dream and a goal?

2. How do you feel when you achieve a goal you have set for yourself?

3. How do you feel when you don't achieve a goal you've set for yourself? What can such an experience teach you?

QUESTION OUTLINE TO GUIDE THE LESSON

1. Why do you think some people are more active than others?

2. Do you think people are more active while they are teenagers, or once they leave school and begin working? Take a guess at the following: ____ out of every 100 teens do no physical activity (Answer: 14; ____ out of every 100 adults do no physical activity. (Answer: 40)

3. People can be placed into one of five stages in terms of their physical activity behaviors: *couch potato* describes people in the first stage; *active exerciser* describes people in the fifth stage. Can you speculate on what might characterize the other three stages?

4. The Physical Activity Pyramid shows different kinds of activity. The stage of behavior you are in is dependent on the kind of activity you are talking about. Look at the Active Sports and Recreation level of the Physical Activity Pyramid. What stage do you think many teenagers are in, if you evaluate them within the Active Sports and Recreation level?

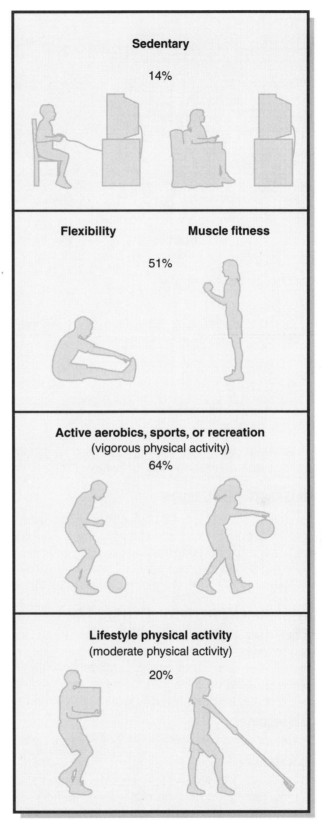

Percentage of teens classified as active exercisers for each of the different types of physical activity.

Five stages of physical activity behavior.

5. What do you think is meant by the term *self-management*?

6. How do self-management skills relate to physical activity behaviors?

7. What are some essential things people with good self-management skills do?

8. As you know, when learning sports skills, practice makes perfect. If you practice the right skills correctly, you'll get better at playing the sport. Is the same true for self-management skills? What might you need to practice to get better at self-management?

9. How can good self-management skills enable you to move to a more active stage of physical activity behavior?

CLOSING DISCUSSION

Review with the class key facts about what happens to physical activity participation as people get older. Reinforce students' understanding of the five stages of physical activity behavior and how each stage differs depending on the kind of activity referred to. Finish by highlighting the new concept, self-management skills. Emphasize the relationship between good self-management skills and lifetime physical activity behaviors.

ENRICHMENT ACTIVITY: FITNESS TRAIL

When they reach adulthood, your students will face many obstacles in their ability to self-manage their physical activity. Certainly one such barrier will be gaining access to exercise venues when traveling, either for work or vacation. More and more hotels are offering fitness trails for guests. These trails provide a good way for people to stay active while on the road. In this activity students learn how to take advantage of fitness trails.

Objectives

For students to perform a complete workout on a fitness trail.

Equipment

The following equipment is needed for the stations described on the Fitness Trail Station Signs. You can modify the stations and worksheet as needed to fit your situation.

- 1 yardstick, for back-saver sit-and-reach
- 1 12-inch-high box, for back-saver sit-and-reach
- 2 posts, driven into ground

- Hula hoops, enough to make hop-scotch course (could instead draw course on ground)
- 1 chin-up bar
- 1 sloping bar
- 1 log or bar, for curl-ups
- 3 bars of three different heights, for push-ups
- 1 slant board
- 1 tree or post, to lean against for calf stretcher

Procedure

1. Before class, place an identifying sign (a Fitness Trail Station Sign) and necessary equipment at each station.

2. Divide the class into 14 groups, or the number of stations you have. Assign each group a starting station.

3. Have groups follow the instructions on their sheets to complete the fitness trail, rotating through all of the stations.

4. Have students cool down after completing the fitness trail.

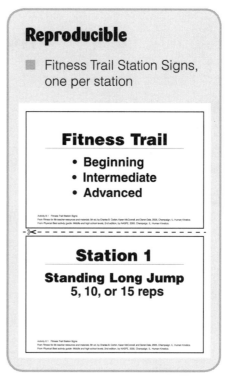

Reproducible

- Fitness Trail Station Signs, one per station

Fitness Trail

- Beginning
- Intermediate
- Advanced

Activity 6.1 Fitness Trail Station Signs
From Fitness for life teacher resources and materials, 5th ed. by Charles B. Corbin, Karen McConnell, and Darren Dale, 2005, Champaign, IL: Human Kinetics.
From Physical Best activity guide: Middle and high school levels, 2nd edition, by NASPE, 2005, Champaign, IL: Human Kinetics.

Station 1

Standing Long Jump
5, 10, or 15 reps

Activity 6.1 Fitness Trail Station Signs
From Fitness for life teacher resources and materials, 5th ed. by Charles B. Corbin, Karen McConnell, and Darren Dale, 2005, Champaign, IL: Human Kinetics.
From Physical Best activity guide: Middle and high school levels, 2nd edition, by NASPE, 2005, Champaign, IL: Human Kinetics.

Goal Setting

MIDDLE AND HIGH SCHOOL

CONCEPT

Goal setting—Planning to determine ahead of time what you expect to accomplish and how you can accomplish it.

OBJECTIVES

- Explain how goal setting can help you plan your fitness program.
- Identify some guidelines you should follow when setting goals.

OPENER

Introduce the lesson by using one of the following ideas:

- Have students work individually to write out the goals they have for physical activity, a sport, or other interest area, for six months, one year, and five years beyond this point in time. Ask each student to list three tasks they must do to achieve these goals.

- In small groups, students list features of a good goal (measurable, worthy, achievable, has a time line).

- In small groups, students think of a sports player or media personality and then create a list of the goals this person may have written down five years ago.

- For the entire class, create a "nonsense" set of goals on the board and have students critique and refine these goals to make them more realistic, with a better time frame, more measurable, and so forth.

- Both reproducibles should be handed out to students to use as a reference as they are writing their own goals.

Reproducibles

- Setting Goals, one per student
- Short-Term Versus Long-Term Goals, one per student

QUESTION OUTLINE TO GUIDE THE LESSON

(Teachers: For more information on this topic, see pages 84-85 of the *Fitness For Life* student textbook.)

1. Explain how successful people use goal setting to achieve something they deem important.

2. What are the differences between short-term and long-term goals?

3. What are the important things to remember about setting a long-term physical activity goal?

4. Explain whether it is necessary to set long-term goals to improve your fitness, and why.

5. Why do experts recommend writing down your long-term fitness goals?

6. Often, a pad and paper is all some people need to list their long-term goals. What electronic devices are also available to help you with goal setting? What is an advantage of these electronic devices? What is a disadvantage?

7. What are the characteristics of short-term goals?

8. What is an example of a short-term physical activity goal?

9. What might be a problem with listing "improving your fitness" as a short-term goal?

10. What is the best way of using short-term goals to improve your fitness?

11. What are some general guidelines for setting physical activity goals?

12. List some additional guidelines for people with different levels of physical activity goal-setting experience: beginners, intermediate, and advanced.

CLOSING DISCUSSION

Emphasize the importance of goal setting as a self-management skill critical to lifetime physical activity behaviors. Review the difference between short-term and long-term goals. Finish by explaining that becoming proficient at goal setting increases the chances of becoming successful in physical activity and other areas of life.

ENRICHMENT ACTIVITY: SCHOOL STEPPING

Objective

This activity will help students become familiar with using a pedometer to better understand how stepping goals relate to physical activity recommendations.

Equipment

Pedometers (optional), 1 per student

Procedure

1. Give each student a School Stepping worksheet and a pedometer.

2. Help students to set and test their pedometers to make sure they are functioning properly.

Digital Vision

3. Explain the instructions for completing the worksheet. Tell students that this activity will give them practice at managing their own participation in physical activity.

4. To extend this activity, have students set specific goals for improvement and continue to count steps throughout the unit or semester, recording their steps as they go. Then at the end of the unit or semester they could evaluate the improvements they've made. Through this experience, they'll gain valuable practice in goal setting and self-management.

Reproducible

■ School Stepping

Name: _____ Class: _____ Date: _____

Activity 8.2
School Stepping

School Stepping is designed to help you become familiar with using a pedometer to better understand how stepping goals relate to physical activity recommendations. Work in a small group to complete the challenges described below. Keep track of the steps you complete during each challenge to see which ones require the most steps. Try to complete as many challenges as you can. If you complete the challenges below, create your own challenges to try.

Walk
Walk around a track or field for 3 minutes.

Jog
Jog around a track or field for 3 minutes.

Jump Rope
Jump rope for 3 minutes, resting as needed.

Grapevine
Grapevine around a track or field for 3 minutes. Switch between right and left sides.

Spring and Walk
Spring for 100 yards and then walk for 100 years. Repeat for a total of 3 minutes.

Walk the Stairs
Walk up and down a flight of stairs for 3 minutes.

Tag
Play a game of tag for 3 minutes. Determine boundaries for your games before you start.

Activity 8.2 School Stepping
From Fitness for life teacher resources and materials, 5th ed. by Charles B. Corbin, Karen McConnell, and Darren Dale. 2005, Champaign, IL Human Kinetics.
From Physical Best activity guide: Middle and high school levels, 2nd edition, by NASPE, 2005, Champaign, IL Human Kinetics.

CHAPTER

9

Being a Good Physical Activity Consumer

© Human Kinetics

Your students have probably seen and heard newspaper, magazine, radio, and television advertisements for health and fitness products and services. But do they have the knowledge to tell if a product or service is really safe and effective? In this chapter we provide lessons, resource materials, and activities that will help your students learn how to become wise purchasers and consumers of health and fitness products.

Activities

Chapter 9 Activities Grid

Activity number	Activity title	Activity page	Concept	Middle school	High school	Reproducible (on CD-ROM)
9.1	Health and Fitness Quackery	179	Quackery and passive exercise	●	●	Evaluating Exercise Devices
						Fitness-Related Experts
9.2	Evaluating Health Products	181	Quackery and self-motivated exercise	●	●	Sense and Nonsense
						Evaluating Health and Fitness Information and Services
	Enrichment Activity: Exercise at Home	182	Exercise	●	●	Exercising at Home

9.1 — Health and Fitness Quackery

MIDDLE AND HIGH SCHOOL

CONCEPTS

- **Quackery**—A method of advertising or selling that uses false claims to lure people into buying products that are worthless or even harmful.
- **Passive exercise**—Being moved by a machine rather than using your own muscles to produce movement.

OBJECTIVES

- Explain the importance of being an informed health consumer.
- Name reliable sources of health-related and fitness-related information.
- Name and describe examples of health-related and fitness-related misconceptions and quackery.

OPENER

Introduce the lesson by using one of the following ideas:

- For the entire class, elicit ideas about why people are uninformed about fitness, health, and wellness.
- In small groups, have students list the best places for finding information about health and fitness. Ask students why they believe the sources they identified are the best.
- In small groups have students list the most outrageous claims they know of pertaining to fitness and dietary products and services.

Reproducibles

- Evaluating Exercise Devices, one per student
- Fitness-Related Experts, one per student

Activity 9.1
Evaluating Exercise Devices

Objective: To evaluate an exercise device.

Procedure:
1. Select the exercise device you will be evaluating and complete the requested information about the product.
2. Place an "X" in each box that applies to your product.
3. Total up the number of marks for your product. The higher the score, the more likely the product is safe and effective.
4. Answer the questions.

"X"	Evaluation	
	The exercise device requires effort and is not passive.	Name of device:
	The exercise device is safe and the exercise done using it is safe.	Description of device:
	The device is fun to use.	
	There are not claims that appear to be quackery.	
	The seller has sound credentials.	
	The product does something for you that is otherwise not possible.	
	The device can be returned for a refund.	
	The cost of the product is reasonable and justifiable.	Manufacturer of device:
	The device is easy to put together, store, and maintain.	
	The device comes with a warranty against defects.	

1. Is the device you evaluated safe? Why or why not?
2. What changes could be made to make the device safer to use?
3. Do you think the device you evaluated would do what it claims to do?
4. How might you change either the device or the instructions to make it more effective?

Activity 9.1
Fitness-Related Experts

Title	Description
Physician with legitimate credentials (MD or DO)	Expert in diagnosis and treatment of injury and illness.
Registered nurse (RN)	Expert in administering medical treatment and health care services.
Certified health education teacher	Expert in health education and health-related issues.
Physical educator	Expert in exercise, sport, dance, and physical fitness.
Registered physical therapist (RPT)	Expert in rehabilitation through exercise, massage, heat, cold, sound, electrical stimulus, gait training, and other modalities.
Registered dietitian (RD)	Expert on food and nutrition.

TARGET QUESTIONS

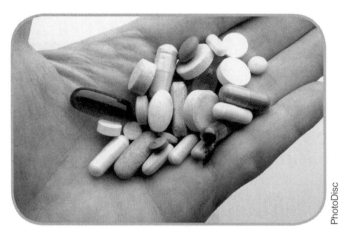

1. You are watching television and your favorite actress shows up in a weight-loss advertisement. She claims that she lost all of her weight fast by using a product. How would you respond?

2. Name a favorite magazine you like to read. What types of health and fitness products are advertised in that magazine? What "red flags" should you look for when evaluating those product ads?

Note: Furnish reproducibles to students to use as a reference tool during this lesson.

QUESTION OUTLINE TO GUIDE THE LESSON

1. What is meant by the term *quackery?*
2. Why do people become victims of quackery?
3. How can you detect quackery and fraud when evaluating claims for exercise and nutritional products?
4. What do you have to be aware of when assessing the credentials of a person making a claim about a product?
5. If you are seeking nutrition advice from a health professional or someone advertising a product, what credentials should you look for? (Teacher note: If you want to learn about good nutrition you need to consider the source of that information in regards to how qualified that source is to offer sound advice.)
6. What does the term *discrediting* mean? How is it used in the selling of exercise and nutritional products?
7. Exaggerated claims about a product appear in advertising and on the product packaging. What are some examples of false promises made in marketing?
8. What claims are made about nutritional supplements?
9. Why should you be wary about claims made by many manufacturers of nutritional supplements?
10. What claims are made about sports supplements, and why should you be wary?
11. What is a fad diet?
12. Explain why spot reducing and passive exercise machines are considered fitness quackery.

CLOSING DISCUSSION

Review what is meant by the term *fitness quackery*. Ask students for reasons why quackery is so prevalent. Emphasize the importance of evaluating the credentials of the people making claims about products and services. Review many of the standard claims and false promises used to sell products and services. Ask students to provide brief examples of claims for specific products. Finish by reviewing reasons why specific claims that constitute fitness quackery continue to persist.

9.2 Evaluating Health Products

MIDDLE AND HIGH SCHOOL

CONCEPTS

- **Quackery**—A method of advertising or selling that uses false claims to lure people into buying products that are worthless or even harmful.
- **Self-motivated exercise**—Becoming more physically active due to a personal need or desire to do so.

OBJECTIVES

- Evaluate health-related and fitness-related facilities.
- Describe the proper clothing and equipment that you need for physical activity.
- Evaluate printed material, videos, and Internet resources related to health and fitness.

OPENER

Introduce the lesson by using one of the following ideas:

- For the entire class, ask students to provide examples of products and services marketed by the exercise and diet industry. Through guided discussion, ask whether these products are effective or not and why.
- In small groups, ask students to list criteria they would use to determine whether a product or service has merit.
- Provide small groups with photos of advertisements for products and services. In their small groups, the students red-flag buzzwords and marketing strategies that the ads use to help sell products.

Reproducibles

- Sense and Nonsense, one per student

  The answers for Sense and Nonsense are: 1-N, 2-N, 3-N, 4-N, 5-S, 6-N, 7-N, 8-N, 9-S, 10-N, 11-N, 12-N, 13-S, 14-N, 15-N, 16-S, 17-N, 18-N, 19-N, 20-N, 21-S, 22-N, 23-N, 24-N, 25-S

- Evaluating Health and Fitness Information and Services, one per student

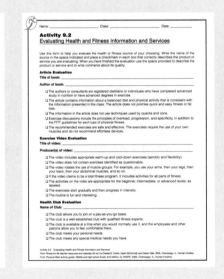

Photo by Dan Wendt

QUESTION OUTLINE TO GUIDE THE LESSON

1. What are the advantages of joining a fitness center or health club?

2. It is not necessary to join a health club in order to be active. What are some lower-cost alternatives to more expensive health clubs?

3. What are guidelines to keep in mind when considering joining a commercial health club?

4. Why should you make a trial visit to a health club you are considering joining?

5. What are some guidelines for selecting clothing and shoes for physical activity?

6. What types of exercise equipment are available to use in the home?

7. What do you need to consider if buying exercise equipment to use at home?

8. What guidelines should you consider when evaluating a book or article about exercise?

9. What guidelines should you consider when evaluating a book about nutrition and health?

10. What guidelines should you consider when evaluating the value of an exercise video?

11. How can you evaluate information on the Internet?

12. What are examples of reputable agencies and organizations for health, physical activity, and nutrition?

ENRICHMENT ACTIVITY: EXERCISE AT HOME

Objectives

Students will perform health-related fitness exercises using common household items. Students will learn that there is a wide variety of ways to exercise and that they do not have to pay a lot of money for equipment and programs advertised on television to get a good workout.

Equipment

The following equipment is needed for the stations described on the Exercising at Home Worksheet. You can modify the stations and worksheet as needed to fit your situation.

- Several small benches or steps, for stair stepping
- Bleachers (preferable) or several benches or steps, for step push-up
- Several towels, enough for use at four stations
- Several broomsticks, enough for use at four stations
- 20 or more food cans of various sizes, for use at two stations
- Several jump ropes
- CD player and music

Opener

1. Place a sign and equipment at each station.
2. Have students do a warm-up.
3. After the warm-up, hand out the Exercising at Home worksheet to each student.
4. Divide the class into five groups, one for each station. Assign each group a station.
5. Have the students divide equally among the different exercises at each station. Have students read the directions and then practice the assigned exercise.
6. One student from each exercise will demonstrate that exercise to the class.
7. Have each group return to their starting station and perform the assigned exercise.
8. On a signal, have groups rotate to the next station.
9. After all students have had a chance to use each of the five types of exercise "equipment," have students cool-down.

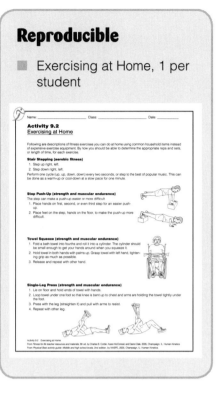

Reproducible

- Exercising at Home, 1 per student

CLOSING DISCUSSION

Review the guidelines students should follow if choosing a health club to join. Ask students what they would evaluate on a trial visit to a health club. Review the wide variety of home exercise equipment available and highlight the advantages and disadvantages of home exercise. Review what to look for when evaluating books and articles, videos, and the Internet. Finally, provide Web sites of reputable associations for health, physical activity, and nutrition.

CHAPTER

10

Planning for a Physically Active Lifestyle

© Human Kinetics

Once your students graduate they will be on their own—you'll no longer be there to help them stay physically active. Therefore, it's crucial that you prepare your students to plan their own physically active lifestyle. The lesson plans, resource materials, and activities in this chapter will help your students learn to plan their personal physical activity programs and learn how to stay active throughout their lives.

Activities

Chapter 10 Activities Grid

Activity number	Activity title	Activity page	Concept	Middle school	High school	Reproducible (on CD-ROM)
10.1	Program Planning	187	Fitness profile	●	●	Developing Your Personal Plan
10.2	Sticking to a Plan	189	Nonactive versus physically active	●	●	Personal Exercise Word Puzzle
						Fitness Review Crossword Puzzle
						Overcoming Barriers
10.3	Evaluating a Physical Activity Program	192	Evaluation	●	●	Reproducibles for this activity are specific to each Self-Assessment or Activity Idea.
	Self-Assessment Idea: Evaluating Your Physical Activity Program	192	Evaluation	●	●	Evaluating Your Physical Activity Program
	Activity Idea: Perform Your Plan	192	Evaluation and change	●	●	Performing Your Plan
	Activity Idea: Your Exercise Circuit	193	Development	●	●	Your Exercise Circuit
	Activity Idea: Your Health and Fitness Club	194	Evaluation	●	●	Your Health and Fitness Club
	Activity Idea: Heart Rate Target Zones	195	Heart rate and aerobic fitness		●	Aerobic Fitness: How Much Activity Is Enough?
	Activity Idea: Sports Stars	196	Exercise	●	●	Sports Stars Program

10.1 Program Planning

MIDDLE AND HIGH SCHOOL

CONCEPT

Fitness profile—A summary of the results of self-assessments of several different components of fitness.

OBJECTIVES

- Explain how to use a fitness profile to plan a personal fitness program.
- Describe the five steps in planning a personal fitness program.

OPENER

Introduce the lesson by using one of the following ideas:

- In small groups, ask students to create a fitness profile. Have different small groups create a fitness profile for an athlete, an unfit teen, and a middle-aged person. Guide the discussion about components to include in a fitness profile.
- For the entire class, elicit a list of things to consider when planning a personal fitness program. Categorize the class responses, for example into personal, social, affective, environmental, and time considerations.

QUESTION OUTLINE TO GUIDE THE LESSON

Have the students use the reproducible handout as a reference tool during this activity.

1. What is a fitness profile and how is a fitness profile used?
2. What health-related fitness components are included in a fitness profile?
3. Which activities in a fitness profile have both upper body and lower body ratings?
4. How is a physical activity profile used?
5. What questions might appear on a physical activity profile?
6. How can you use the Physical Activity Pyramid to help make improvements to your physical activity profile? (Physical Activity Pyramid appears as reproducible for Activity 8.1 on CD-ROM).
7. What are some examples of goals teens might have for exercise and physical activity?
8. How should the goals of a beginner differ from the goals of someone who is more advanced?

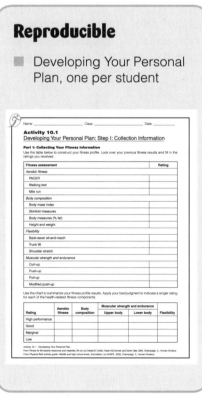

Reproducible

- Developing Your Personal Plan, one per student

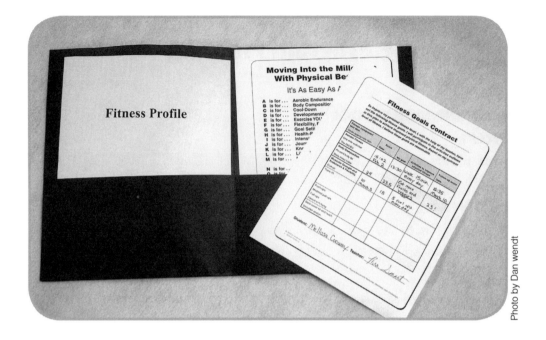

Photo by Dan Wendt

9. What guidelines should a person follow when goal setting for physical activity?

10. What factors should you consider when planning activities for different days of the week?

CLOSING DISCUSSION

Review the fitness profile, using an example to show to the class. Highlight the key features of a fitness profile, pointing out the areas of health-related fitness that might need improving. Comment on the difference between a fitness profile and a physical activity profile. Review the guidelines to follow when setting physical activity goals. Finish by emphasizing the connection between program planning and goal setting: A sound program will lead to achievement of realistic goals.

10.2 **Sticking to a Plan**

MIDDLE AND HIGH SCHOOL

CONCEPT

Nonactive versus physically active—A person who is sedentary or does no physical activity versus a person who is physically active.

OBJECTIVES

- Describe the five stages of physical activity.
- Identify the strategies that help people become active and stay active at each of the stages.

OPENER

Introduce the lesson by using one of the following ideas:

- In small groups, ask students why they think some people choose to be couch potatoes while other people choose to be physically active.
- In small groups, ask students to create a physical activity promotion brochure or poster targeted at people who are sedentary, or have different groups create brochures aimed at people at different levels of change.
- In small groups, ask students to speculate on why people discontinue physical activity and what might be done to prevent people from discontinuing.

Reproducibles

- Personal Exercise Word Puzzle
- Fitness Review Crossword Puzzle (answers at end of activity)
- Overcoming Barriers

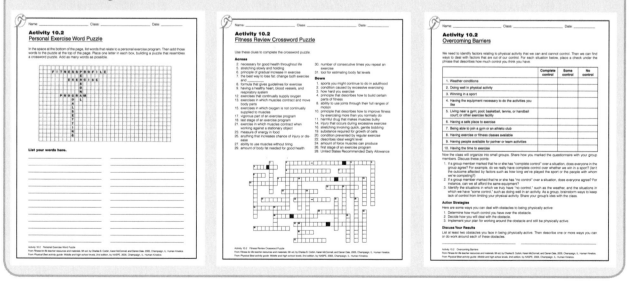

QUESTION OUTLINE TO GUIDE THE LESSON

1. Some people are very active while some choose to be sedentary. What are the five stages of physical activity behavior? (introduced in Activity 8.1)

2. If people do sports in school, how likely is it that they will continue to be physically active once they leave school?

3. What are some strategies that can help people who are couch potatoes become more active?

4. What beliefs and attitudes do couch potatoes hold that influence their behaviors?

5. What strategies can motivate people who are thinking about being active to begin a physical activity program?

6. What is the difference between self-perception and self-confidence?

7. People who are planning to be physically active can benefit from strategies appropriate to people in earlier stages. What additional strategies would also be helpful?

8. How can a personal digital assistant (PDA) be used to help a person increase physical activity participation?

9. What strategies are appropriate for people who are physically active on an intermittent basis?

10. Some people can be considered "active for life." What strategies should these people use to help keep active?

CLOSING DISCUSSION

Review the five stages of physical activity involvement. Review the strategies appropriate for each stage that are designed to move individuals to the next, more active, stage.

FITNESS REVIEW CROSSWORD PUZZLE ANSWERS

Across

2. health-related fitness
5. static
6. progression
7. diet
8. FITT
9. cardiovascular fitness
12. aerobic
13. isotonic
15. anaerobic
17. workout
18. cool-down
21. isometric
23. calorie
25. risk factor
27. muscular endurance
29. essential
30. reps
31. calipers

Down

1. lifetime
2. hyperkinetic
3. intensity
4. specificity
8. flexibility
10. overload
11. steroid
14. overuse
16. ballistic
19. nutrient
20. hypokinetic
22. target
24. strength
26. warm-up
28. USRDA

10.3 Evaluating a Physical Activity Program

MIDDLE AND HIGH SCHOOL LEVELS

SELF-ASSESSMENT IDEA: Evaluating Your Physical Activity Program

Objective

Students will perform activities from their own physical activity plan and complete a worksheet evaluating their plan.

Equipment

Select equipment needed by students for their activities. Well before teaching this lesson, you'll need to discuss students' physical activity plans to find out what types of activities students will likely want to participate in during the lesson. Their activity ideas will dictate the equipment needs.

Procedure

1. Have students perform a warm-up.

2. Have students select one day from their activity plan and perform as many of the activities as possible in class. If no single day's activities last as long as one class period, they should supplement their workout with activities from another day on their plan. If equipment is not available, students should select an activity that is similar in its benefits and one that they will likely enjoy.

3. Students should perform activities in their plan that are not completed in class at appropriate times of the day.

4. On the following day students should use the Evaluating Your Physical Activity Program worksheet to evaluate their plan. Students should record the activities they were able to complete.

5. Students should record reasons to explain the activities that were not completed (for example, bad weather, homework).

Assessment

Have students put their recorded results in their portfolios or a folder or turn them in to you for safekeeping.

ACTIVITY IDEA: Perform Your Plan

Objective

For students to modify one day of their personal program plan based upon results from the previous lesson (Self-Assessment Idea: Evaluating Your Physical Activity Program).

Reproducible

- Evaluating Your Physical Activity Program

Equipment

Select equipment needed by students for their activities. Well before teaching this lesson, you'll need to discuss students' physical activity plans to find out what types of activities students will likely want to participate in during the lesson. Their activity ideas will dictate the equipment needs.

Procedure

1. This lesson is similar to the previous lesson, Self-Assessment Idea: Evaluating Your Physical Activity Program. After students have completed the previous lesson and evaluated their plans, have them decide how they should change their plans based on their evaluation.

2. Have students perform the same activity plan with any modifications made as a result of their program evaluation.

3. Alternatively, students may choose to perform activities from a different day of their plan.

ACTIVITY IDEA: YOUR EXERCISE CIRCUIT

Objectives

Students will plan a total fitness exercise circuit. This activity will help prepare students for planning their own activity programs in the future.

Equipment

- CD player and music
- Several sheets of blank paper and pencils at each of four stations
- Use available equipment to create four stations for each of the fitness areas:
  1. Aerobic fitness
  2. Muscular strength and endurance (upper body)
  3. Muscular strength and endurance (lower body)
  4. Flexibility

Procedure

1. Have students perform a warm-up.
2. Give each student a Your Exercise Circuit handout.
3. Divide the class into eight groups (two groups will go to each of the four stations).
4. Assign each group a station.

Reproducible

- Performing Your Plan

Reproducible

- Your Exercise Circuit, one per student

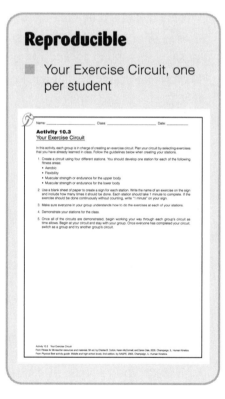

5. Have each group create one station for the circuit (have them create a sign for their station with the name of an appropriate exercise on the sign and a number of times it should be done). After the first round, you should have two exercises at each station.

6. Have each group demonstrate their exercise to the class.

7. Have each group return to their starting station and perform the assigned exercise.

8. On a signal, have groups rotate to the next station.

9. After students have completed all four stations, have them stay in their groups, but send them to a different station than the one they started with last time. Have them create a new circuit (with new exercises), and repeat the activity.

10. Have students cool-down as a large group.

ACTIVITY IDEA: YOUR HEALTH AND FITNESS CLUB

Objective

To practice evaluating services and the quality of a health club, by creating a health and fitness club at school. Students will perform activities in the mock student health and fitness club you've created. This will help them prepare for doing this on their own in the future.

Equipment

- Exercise equipment as needed for exercise stations (see instructions below)
- Poster board, at least eight sheets
- Markers, plenty for all eight groups
- Pens and pencils, at least 1 per student
- CD player and music

Procedure

1. Give each student a Your Health and Fitness Club worksheet.

2. Have them do the group planning (part I of the worksheet).

3. In small groups, have students set up their activity stations.

4. Allow each group two to three minutes to describe the activities they have planned.

5. Allow students to freely move from station to station performing the created activities.

6. Have one or two students remain at their own station to explain and demonstrate the activities to other groups.

7. Rotate who remains at the stations so that all students have a chance to be a demonstrator.

8. Have students record their performances at each station (part II of the worksheet).

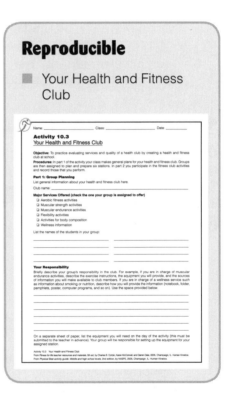

Reproducible

■ Your Health and Fitness Club

ACTIVITY IDEA: Heart Rate Target Zones (use for High School Level only)

Objective

Students will determine how much physical activity is needed for aerobic fitness. This information is helpful for future program planning by your students.

Equipment

- Badminton net, rackets, and birdies
- Volleyball net and ball
- Basketball

Procedure

1. Mark the walking and jogging paths. Set up badminton, volleyball, and basketball areas.

2. Have students perform a warm-up.

3. After the warm-up, give each student an Aerobic Fitness: How Much Activity Is Enough? worksheet.

4. Review with students the correct procedure for counting heart rate. Tell students to calculate their resting heart rate and record the results.

5. Have students follow the directions in part I of the worksheet to calculate their target heart rate zone, using both the heart rate range method and the percentage of maximal heart rate. Have students record their results.

6. For part II, divide the class in half and have them perform each of the jogging and walking activities (five minutes each).

7. Ask students to determine their heart rate and record this. Have students determine if they exceeded their target heart rate.

8. Tell students to follow directions in part III of the worksheet. Here, students can select activities (badminton, volleyball, basketball, jogging) to perform to reach a caloric expenditure of 200 calories. Students attempt to reach the 200-calorie goal by adding the calories from walking and jogging to the calories they will expend in their chosen activity in part III.

9. Have students cool down by performing some static stretching.

Reproducible

- Aerobic Fitness: How Much Activity Is Enough?

ACTIVITY IDEA: SPORTS STARS

Objective

Students can earn stars by participating in sports. This helps students take responsibility for finding their own activities to participate in outside of class.

Equipment

Gather equipment for the activities you choose to play in class.

Procedure

1. Give each student a Sports Stars Program worksheet. Have them fill in part I during the course of a week.

2. One week later, refer students to their worksheets again. Tell students to make a plan for the following week incorporating changes that might help them reach their goals. Students should use the chart in part II to indicate which sports they will perform over the next week.

3. After students are done planning their week, tell them that today they are going to earn stars in class by playing a sports activity. They will earn more stars by participating in activities outside of class. They can use this activity time to start fulfilling the plan they created in part II of the worksheet.

4. Have students perform a warm-up.

5. Have students choose and play a sports activity. Students should keep track of playing time and compare it to part II of the worksheet.

6. Have students cool-down after activity.

7. Tell them to record the number of stars they earned in class.

8. Ask students to earn their remaining stars by the end of the week.

Assessment

Have students put their recorded results in their portfolios or a folder or turn them in to you for safekeeping.

Reproducible

Sports Stars Program

REFERENCES

Alter, M.J. 1998. *Sport stretch*, 2nd ed. Champaign, IL: Human Kinetics.

American Academy of Pediatrics (AAP) Committee on Sports Medicine and Fitness. 2001. Policy statement: Strength training by children and adolescents. *Pediatrics* 107(6): 1470-72.

American College of Sports Medicine (ACSM). 2000. *ACSM's guidelines for exercise testing and prescription*, 6th ed. Philadelphia: Lippincott, Williams, and Wilkins.

Bar-Or, O., and R.M. Malina. 1995. Activity, health and fitness of children and adolescents. In *Child health, nutrition, and physical activity*, ed. L.W.Y. Cheung and J.B. Richmond, 79-123. Champaign, IL: Human Kinetics.

Blair, S.N., H.W. Kohl, 3rd, C.E. Barlow, R.S. Paffenbarger, Jr., L.W. Gibbons, C.A. Macera. 1995. Changes in physical fitness and all-cause mortality: A prospective study of healthy and unhealthy men. *Journal of the American Medical Association* 273: 1093-98.

Blanchard, Y. 1999. Health-Related Fitness for Children and Adults with Cerebral Palsy. *American College of Sports Medicine current comment*, August.

Bompa, T.O. 2000. *Total training for young champions*. Champaign, IL: Human Kinetics.

Boreham, C.A., J. Twisk, L. Murray, M. Savage, J.J. Strain, and G.W. Cran. 2001. Fitness, fatness, and coronary heart disease risk in adolescents: The Northern Ireland Young Hearts Project. *Medicine and science in sports and exercise* 33: 270-74.

Boreham, C.A., J. Twisk, M. Savage, G.W. Cran, and J.J. Strain. 1997. Physical activity, sports participation, and risk factors in adolescents. *Medicine and science in sports and exercise* 29: 788-93.

Borg, G. 1998. *Borg's perceived exertion and pain scales*. Champaign, IL: Human Kinetics.

California Department of Education. 2002. State study proves physically fit kids perform better academically. www.cde.ca.gov/news/releases2002/rel37.asp

Cooper Institute. 2004. *FITNESSGRAM/ACTIVITYGRAM test administration manual*, 2nd ed. Champaign, IL: Human Kinetics.

Corbin, C.B., and R.P. Pangrazi. 2002. Physical activity for children: How much is enough? In *FITNESSGRAM reference guide*, ed. G.J. Welk, R.J. Morrow, and H.B. Falls (p. 7, Internet Resource). Dallas: The Cooper Institute.

Corbin, C.B. and R. Lindsey. 2005. *Fitness for life*. 5th ed. Champaign, IL: Human Kinetics.

Darst, P. and R. Pangrazi. 2002. *Dynamic physical education for secondary school students*. 4th ed. San Francisco: Benjamin Cummins.

Darst, P., R. Pangrazi, and B. Stillwell. 1995. Middle school physical education: Make it more exciting. *Journal of physical education, recreation, and dance* 66(8): 8-9.

Faigenbaum, A., and W. Westcott. 2000. *Strength and power for young athletes*. Champaign, IL: Human Kinetics.

Hass, C.J., M.S. Feigenbaum, and B.A. Franklin. 2001. Prescription of resistance training for healthy populations. *Sports medicine* 31(14): 953-964.

Heyward, V.H. 2002. *Advanced fitness assessment and exercise prescription*. 4th ed. Champaign, IL: Human Kinetics.

Joint Committee on National Health Education Standards. 1995. *National health education standards: Achieving health literacy*. Atlanta: American Cancer Society.

Knudson, D.V., P. Magnusson, and M. McHugh. June 2000. Current issues in flexibility fitness. In *The President's Council on physical fitness and sports digest*, series 3, no. 10, ed. C. Corbin and B. Pangrazi, 1-8. Washington, DC: Department of Health and Human Services.

Kraemer, W.J. and S.J. Fleck. 1993. *Strength training for young adults*. Champaign, IL: Human Kinetics.

National Association for Sport and Physical Education (NASPE). 2004a. *Moving into the future: National standards for physical education*, 2nd ed. Reston, VA: Author.

National Association for Sport and Physical Education (NASPE). 1992. *Outcomes of quality physical education programs*. Reston, VA: Author.

National Association for Sport and Physical Education (NASPE). 2004b. *Physical activity for children: A statement of guidelines for children ages 5-12*, 2nd ed. Reston, VA: Author.

National Dance Association (NDA). 1996. *National standards for dance education: What every young American should know and be able to do in dance* . Reston, VA: Author.

National Strength and Conditioning Association (NSCA). 1985. Position statement on prepubescent strength training. *National strength and conditioning association journal* 7: 27-31.

Rowland, T.W. 1996. *Developmental exercise physiology.* Champaign, IL: Human Kinetics.

Sothern, M.S., M. Loftin, R.M. Suskind, J.N. Udall, and U. Becker. 1999. The health benefits of physical activity in children and adolescents: Implications for chronic disease prevention. *European journal of pediatrics* 158: 271-74.

Tanaka, H., K.D. Monahan, and D.R. Seals. 2001. Age-predicted maximal heart rate revisited. *Journal of the American College of Cardiology* 37(1): 153-56.

U.S. Department of Health and Human Services (USDHHS). 1996. *Physical activity and health: A report of the Surgeon General.* U.S. Department of Health and Human Services, Centers for Disease Control and Prevention, National Center for Chronic Disease Prevention and Health Promotion. Atlanta, GA: U.S. Department of Health and Human Services, Government Printing Office.

Weiss, Maureen. 2000. *Motivating kids in physical activity.* President's Council on Physical Fitness and Sports. SuDocHE 20.114:3/11.

Winnick, J.P. and F.X. Short, eds. 1999. *The Brockport physical fitness training guide.* Champaign, IL: Human Kinetics.

Xiang, P., R. McBride, J. Guan, and M. Solomon. 2003. Children's motivation in elementary physical education: An expectancy-value model of achievement choice. *Research Quarterly for Exercise and Sport* 74(1): 25-35.

ABOUT PHYSICAL BEST

Physical Best is a comprehensive health-related fitness education program developed by physical educators for physical educators. Physical Best was designed to educate, challenge, and encourage all children in the knowledge, skills, and attitudes needed for a healthy and fit life. The goal of the program is to help students move from dependence to independence and responsibility for their own health and fitness by promoting regular, enjoyable physical activity. The purpose of Physical Best is to educate ALL children regardless of athletic talent, physical and mental abilities, or disabilities. This is implemented through quality resources and professional development workshops for physical educators.

Physical Best is a program of the National Association for Sport and Physical Education (NASPE). A nonprofit membership organization of over 18,000 professionals in the sport and physical education fields, NASPE is an association of the American Alliance for Health, Physical Education, Recreation and Dance dedicated to strengthening basic knowledge about healthy lifestyles among professionals and the general public. Putting that knowledge into action in schools and communities across the nation is critical to improved academic performance, social reform, and the health of individuals.